THE FOUNDERS'
SPEECH
TO A NATION IN CRISIS

THE FOUNDERS'
SPEECH
TO A NATION IN CRISIS

STUDENT EDITION

What the Founders
Would Say to America Today

STEVEN RABB

STUDENT EDITION

ISBN

978-1-7358164-5-6

Copyright © 2020 Steven Rabb

Printed by Liberty For All Publishers in the United States

Student Edition Printing, 2023.

Visit

www.TheFoundersUSA.com

to sign up for new release alerts and The Founders USA newsletter.

Liberty For All Publishers

Atlanta, Georgia

*For all the men and women who have fought to defend
our nation and rescue liberty from tyranny.*

*For my sons,
Kevin and Connor*

And for the preservation of liberty for all.

ACKNOWLEDGEMENTS

Without the love and support of my beautiful and loving wife, Shannon, this passion project would never have been completed. Without the encouragement of my amazing sons, Kevin and Connor, it would never have started.

Special thanks to my editor, Jessica Mohr, who went above and beyond to bring this book together. Also special thanks to Kristina Konstantinova for her wonderful work on the formatting, Ghislain Viau for the powerful cover design, Josh Masterson for his contribution to the prologue, Cori Rupe for her excellent consultation, and Shawna Amit for her outstanding management of the pieces and process.

Table of Contents

FOREWORD

Very few pivotal leaders, events, and movements in history have made a dramatic, lasting, and universal impact on the development of human civilization. While the list may be debatable, honest observers would rank the life and death of Jesus of Nazareth at the top of the list. The Gutenberg press would also be a contender for the top spot, as well as the subsequent Reformation and Enlightenment, placing knowledge and Scriptural interpretation directly into the hands of the people. Add in the underpinnings of Greek philosophy, and the recipe for Western civilization is just about complete—a faith moderating man's impulses, and a people empowered by the growing knowledge of their God-given rights.

Yet one ingredient was still missing: a political order capable of protecting these religious and natural rights—the required ingredient for humankind to flourish. This was the state of humanity when the thunderbolt that was the American Founding shook the world. It started with the radical declaration that "all men are created equal," sparking a revolution and summoning a group of men uniquely and providentially gifted to play a momentous role in the development of western civilization and world history. As John Quincy Adams so beautifully stated:

> The Declaration of Independence was
> the first solemn declaration, by a nation,
> of the only legitimate foundation of civil
> government. It was the cornerstone of a
> new fabric, destined to cover the surface

of the globe. It demolished at a stroke the lawfulness of all governments founded upon conquest. It swept away all the rubbish of accumulated centuries of servitude. It announced in practical form to the world the transcendent truth of the inalienable sovereignty of the people.

The sovereignty of the people. A government by their consent. These ideas were gamechangers. But the ideas themselves were not enough. They needed to be inextricably tethered to—unequivocally embedded in—a constitution that would place out of reach the scepter of power, keeping in check the ambitious tyrant lurking within the heart of every man.

In the summer of 1787, these men gathered once again to craft the Constitution of the United States of America, a document of law that would so protect the liberties of the people, so balance and define the limited powers of the federal government, and so affirm the role of states in a republic, it would become the protector of the rights of mankind for generations to come, at home and abroad.

To all who stand in awe of the Founding Fathers' genius, this book will confirm and enhance your appreciation of these incredible men. To all who believe in the providence of a loving God in the lives and affairs of men, this book demonstrates that the Father of our nation shares your deeply held beliefs. To all who cherish our religious and civil rights, this book is a reminder of the liberties fought for and won, and must now be reclaimed. For all the families who have sacrificed loved ones in defense of our nation, this book is a memorial to those patriots who gave the last full measure of devotion for the United States of America. Finally, to all who despair at the current state of America, this book is a call to stand and take action – a call to save the country we love, once again, from the outstretched arm of tyranny.

In the Student Edition of *The Founders' Speech to a Nation in Crisis* the reader will find 530 new endnotes and a thorough bibliography with more than 70 source materials to help provide context and depth to the powerful words presented in this volume. Students can find additional learning resources on our website at www.TheFoundersUSA.com/Student.

Keep the faith,

Steven Rabb

Author's Note

The initial inspiration for this book stemmed from a robust political debate between me and my two adult sons. Wanting to make my case from the Founders' perspective, I dashed to my bookshelf to peruse books on the Founding, soon returning with a stack, each with a piece of the answer. We spent hours that night, as we often do, discussing the affairs of the day and how the Founders would speak to those issues.

Following that conversation, and for my own edification, I determined it would be easier to reference the Founders' ideas if I could pull them from a single source. Having the most relevant words of the Founders in one place would both equip me for the next political discussion with my sons, and inform my public speaking on the topic.

A few months later I gave a presentation on the founding ideals in the words of the Founding Fathers at the Western Conservative Summit in Colorado. Following the positive response, it dawned on me that the presentation of the Founders' words in the form of a speech needed to be a book. I needed to write a relatable and relevant book to a modern audience that could also serve as a single resource for the Founders' thoughts and principles — in their own words.

From my home office in Woodstock, Georgia, I set out to collect and collate the most relevant texts from the Founders' speeches, essays, letters, and the *Federalist Papers*, weaving them into a tapestry of a speech that builds and develops as a narrative. I knew it would take time, but I did not expect to be pulled into a two-year immersion of their texts and, even more surprisingly, into the words of those who inspired them, as well as many they inspired in the generations that followed. But to tell the full story of America, and of the enlightenment of which they were a part, and through which their promise of equality was eventually kept, I needed to include them all. I needed to hear — and wanted to make accessible — the relevance of all of their words to our issues today, as if the Founders had together visited modern-day America, and reconvened to compose a single speech that would recall America to its founding principles.

As I crafted *The Founders' Speech to a Nation in Crisis*, I imagined the readers as an audience, standing in the back of a town hall meeting, or sitting in a church pew listening intently as the Founders' speech was delivered. I pictured "Scribe," as I eventually called him, at the front of the church, narrating the Founders' words with passion, as though speaking them for the first time.

To help the reader follow the speech, I have enumerated and italicized the author of each text in a superscript citation for immediate attribution. Several texts have been mildly curated to support the narrative, for pronoun consistency, and for modern usage standards.

While this book illustrates how the Founding Fathers agreed on the core principles of liberty, it also digs into the disagreements of the Constitutional Convention, as well as the threats of tyranny that soon challenged our fledgling nation in the ensuing years, and continue to challenge our nation to this day. And thus my purpose for this book is to bring to life the ethos and principles of America's founding while reminding us of who we are as Americans — as a nation of citizens with a common history, as a people with a faith-rooted belief in virtue, and as patriots with a shared commitment to liberty. My hope is that Americans may once again revere the miracle of our nation's founding, that we might once again unite around our shared American creed, *E pluribus unum*: Out of many, one.

INTRODUCTION

| GEORGE WASHINGTON The citizens of America, abounding with all the necessaries and conveniences of life, are now acknowledged to be possessed of absolute freedom and independence. They are from this period to be considered as the actors on a most conspicuous theater which seems to be peculiarly designated by Providence for the display of human greatness and felicity. Here they are not only surrounded with everything which can contribute to the completion of private and domestic enjoyment, but Heaven has crowned all its other blessings by giving a fairer opportunity for political happiness than any other nation has ever been favored with.

The foundation of our empire was not laid in the gloomy age of ignorance and superstition, but at an epoch when the rights of mankind were better understood and more clearly defined than at any former period. The free cultivation of letters, the unbounded extension of commerce, the progressive refinement of manners, the growing liberality of sentiment, and above all, the pure and benign light of Revelation, have had ameliorating influence on mankind and increased the blessings of society. At this auspicious period, the United States came into existence as a nation, and if their citizens should not be completely free and happy, the fault will be entirely their own.

Such is our situation, and such are our prospects; but notwithstanding the cup of blessing is thus reached out to us, notwithstanding happiness is ours, if we have a disposition to seize the occasion and make it our own. Yet it appears to me there is an option still left to the United States of America, that it is in their choice, and depends upon their conduct whether they will be respectable and prosperous, or contemptible and miserable as a nation. This is the time of their political probation. This is the moment when the eyes of the whole world are turned upon them. This is the moment to establish or ruin their national character forever. For it is yet to be decided, whether the Revolution must ultimately be considered as a blessing or a curse — a blessing or a curse not to the present age alone, for with our fate will the destiny of unborn millions be involved.

2 *JAMES MADISON* It has ever been the pride and boast of America, that the rights for which she contended were the rights of human nature. By the blessings of the Author of these rights on the means exerted for their defense, they have prevailed against all opposition, and formed the basis of our independent states.

In this view the citizens of the United States are responsible for the greatest trust ever confided to a political society. If justice, good faith, honor, gratitude, and all the other qualities which enable the character of a nation and fulfill the ends of government be the fruits of our establishments, the cause of liberty will acquire a dignity and luster which it has never yet enjoyed, and an example will be set which cannot but have the most favorable influence on the rights of mankind. If on the other side, our governments should be unfortunately blotted with the reverse of these cardinal and essential virtues, the great cause which we have engaged to vindicate will be dishonored and betrayed; the last and fairest experiment in favor of the rights of human nature will be turned against them, and their patrons and friends exposed to be insulted and silenced by the votaries of tyranny and usurpation. 3 *GEORGE WASHINGTON* And regretted would it be were we to neglect the means and to depart from the road which

Providence has pointed us to so plainly. Indeed, I cannot believe it will ever come to pass.

PROLOGUE

SCRIBE Through a cosmic stroke of Providence, the Founding Fathers have been transported across space and time to deliver one final service to their country. The Founders have been called to survey the state of America today and recall its people to their founding principles through the crafting of a single speech.

Once again, they stand outside Independence Hall in Philadelphia. The intervening years have changed its gardens. The flag on its pole has noticeably more stars. And where once its backdrop was clear sky, now buildings of glass and concrete pull the eye.

The Hall itself, however, appears unchanged, its red brick unfaded, its white window casings untarnished.

All of this, together with the beauty of the day, is taken in by the Founders. Respectfully I follow, selected as their humble Scribe, as they enter the Hall by ones and twos — some deep in thought, some in private conversation — stepping once again toward the Assembly Room.

Quietly, I listen to them discuss all they have surveyed: our schools and communities, churches and culture, and economy and governments. Some speak with more energy than others. Some with more awe. But all are equal parts amazed at society's progress, and disturbed at the loss of its liberties.

Their conversations trail off as they file into the Assembly Room, pausing as a group to take in the fond familiarity of the room. Tables and chairs fill it. Cloth drapes partially cover the windows.

Twin fireplaces flank the far wall covered in rich ivory paper and clean white molding.

"Just as it was so long ago," Alexander Hamilton, his blue eyes shining with restrained emotion, says in deferential tones. He looks toward the high ceiling and adds, "Not even the chandelier has changed."

"And yet," Thomas Jefferson — tall, stately and staid, as in his prime — counters, "so much else has."

The seven men continue to stand. They consider the weight of Jefferson's words as they contemplate their surroundings, its history, and their place in both.

"The power man has achieved over matter," Franklin marvels, his eyes staring out the nearest window — and at the inconceivably tall buildings they frame. "The engineering alone… truly I was born too soon," he finishes with a smile at the group.

"You worked your marvels enough," Samuel Adams ribs. "Let these inventors have their day too."

Franklin's grin grows sheepish. Then, his eyes sharpen as he focuses again on the task at hand. "Gentlemen," he says, "it is for us to write something this generation will read. To say something they will hear."

"To that I must object," Hamilton, offended, argues. "The Constitution and Federalist Papers are certainly worth reading."

"No duel with me, Mr. Hamilton," says Franklin. "I only mean to note that this generation of Americans has clearly read neither. So it is for us to reach them, as we did their forefathers so long ago."

Hamilton considers Franklin's words before offering a begrudging, "Sadly, I must agree." At that cue, each of the seven men move to their historic chairs.

Mr. Washington stands alone on the raised platform at the front of the room, his statuesque physique as commanding as ever. He moves behind the dais's long table. His hand rests briefly on the back of his mahogany chair, on the sun-shaped crest which Franklin had once described as a rising sun. He then looks out fondly at his fellow compatriots, and when he sits most follow suit.

Some remain standing though, including John Adams. Before speaking, he surveys the room from above the dark rims of his glasses. "So much that must be said, gentlemen."

"And you would say it better than any, Mr. Adams," Jefferson responds. His chair — a traditional sack-back Windsor — creaks as he eases himself into it.

The discussion begins in earnest then, words exchanged almost faster than I, their Scribe, can write.

James Madison, noticeably shorter and thinner than the rest of the group, leans with his elbows on his own chair's armrests, clears his throat, and waits for all eyes to fall on him. "This speech, gentlemen," he says with clipped, determined, though quiet words, "must be from all of us. One voice. United."

Before he's even finished, Mr. Hamilton, from his place across the room, agrees. "Of course, but not only in our words, but also in the words of the great minds who preceded us, and perhaps from those who followed…"

"Yes yes," John Adams, with his infamous impatience, says.

"Those generations who followed must be heard. So many sacrificed so much that all might be free."

"I presume, Mr. Adams, you refer to our *civil* war," Jefferson replies with biting wit. The room grows quiet as everyone tries to discern whether he means those differences between Adams and himself or the horrible conflict none in the room had lived to see. Jefferson flashes a smile to his old friend and rival, softening his words. "And I agree. They must be heard. Many generations now of patriots have watered the tree of liberty with their blood…"

"The foremost question, gentlemen," Mr. Franklin interrupts. His gray eyes, discomfortingly steady, fall in turn on everyone in the room — even me, their Scribe. "Is not who should be heard, but where to start."

"The Revolution," Samuel Adams says emphatically. His eyes quickly scan the room as if daring anyone to argue. "We must remind the people of the blood spent to purchase their liberty."

"Agreed, Mr. Adams," his cousin John says with placating nods. "Though not only the War of Independence, but also the revolution in the hearts of the American people."

"That must be said, surely," Mr. Madison acknowledges. The rest of the room quiets to hear his words. "But we must start, gentlemen, with the development of Common Law and the philosophical genius that preceded our Constitution."

"Naturally," Mr. Hamilton says, taking to his feet and crossing the room to stand next to Madison and count him an ally. "The people must understand the rule of law and our system of checks and balances…"

"Gentlemen," Washington interrupts. "If I may?" He looks over the room and, taking their quiet for assent, stands.

Those still sitting respectfully take their feet.

John Adams breaks the lengthening silence. "And what are your thoughts, Mr. Washington?" he asks.

With all eyes on him, and the Rising Sun Chair beside him, Washington reaches into the breast pocket of the blue wool uniform he'd taken to later in life. "I humbly beseech you, gentlemen," he says with certain authority, laying his Bible on the table, "to consider beginning here."

The room remains quiet. Each man is deep in thought.

"Of course," Jefferson says in his understated tones. "The God-given rights of mankind."

"The foundation of the rule of law," Madison follows.

Contentious even in agreement, John Adams adds, "What I see, gentlemen, is the virtue of the people."

Mr. Washington steps in, "All true, gentlemen. But first we must remind the people of the spark of divinity within each of them, the dignity bestowed by the benevolent Creator on every human soul. We start in the beginning."

Again, a quiet fills the room as Washington's words sink in.

And again, it's Jefferson who speaks first. "Of course. The beginning," he says, his eyes lost in thought. Then he turns to me and formally asks, "Sir, will you be so kind as to help us record this speech?" With a wry smile at Mr. John Adams, his friend and rival, he adds, "I would hate for anyone again to complain of my handwriting."

Everyone chuckles — Adams the hardest — as they gather round to begin their work.

Pen in hand, I set to continue taking down their words, but am restrained by a hand on my shoulder.

"Not so fast, young man," Mr. Washington says. "For without His blessing, we would not have come this far."

I sheepishly set down my pen and lower my chin as Mr. Washington reminds us in prayer of whose blessings we enjoy.

Over the hours that follow, the Founding Fathers quote philosophers from generations past, friends from their own time, and writings from the great minds of the few generations who followed them.

Disagreement enters the room but exits just as quickly, as does despair. But their passion never wavers, and the hope always returns for the future of the nation they founded and love.

We work with a deep sense of urgency, quotes rolling off their tongues so fast I can barely keep up. And just as the midnight oil burns, the Founding Fathers complete their speech and depart as suddenly as they arrived. And so my friends, my fellow guardians of liberty, it is my great honor as their Scribe, to present the heartfelt emanations of the Founding Fathers: *The Founders' Speech To A Nation In Crisis*.

CHAPTER ONE
LIBERTY

1 GENESIS 1:27 God created man in His own image, in the image of God He created him; male and female He created them. *2 JEREMIAH 1:5* Before I formed you in the womb I knew you, and before you were born, I consecrated you. *3 ISAIAH 49:15-16* I will not forget you. Behold, I have inscribed you on the palms of My hands.

4 1 JOHN 3:1-2 See how great a love the Father has given us, that we would be called children of God; and in fact we are. Beloved, now we are children of God. *5 2 TIMOTHY 1:7* For God has not given us a spirit of timidity, but of power and love and discipline. *6 2 CORINTHIANS 3:17* And where the Spirit of the Lord is, there is liberty. *7 LEVITICUS 25:10* So proclaim liberty throughout all the land to all its inhabitants, *8 LUKE 6:31* and do to others as you would have them do to you.

9 THOMAS JEFFERSON The God who gave us life, gave us liberty at the same time. *10 ALEXANDER HAMILTON* And God has constituted an eternal and immutable law, which is indispensably obligatory upon all mankind, prior to any human institution whatever. This is what is called the law of nature. Upon this law depends the natural rights of mankind.

11 THOMAS JEFFERSON Under the law of nature, we are all born free, every one comes into the world with a right to their own person, which includes the liberty of moving and using it at their own will. This is your personal liberty and is given to all of us by the Author of nature.

12 PATRICK HENRY All of mankind is by nature free and independent, and each has certain inherent rights. *13 SAMUEL ADAMS* Among the natural rights of man are first, a right to life; secondly, the right to liberty; and thirdly, the right to property, all together with the right to defend them in the best manner we can.

14 FREDERIC BASTIAT Life, liberty, and property do not exist because

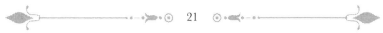

men have made laws. On the contrary, it was the fact that life, liberty, and property existed beforehand that caused men to make laws in the first place.

15 *THOMAS JEFFERSON* A free people claim their rights, as derived from the laws of nature, and not as the gift of their chief magistrate; 16 *DECLARATION OF INDEPENDENCE* To assume among the powers of the earth, the separate and equal station to which the Laws of Nature and of Nature's God entitle them. 17 *HENRY WARD BEECHER* For the real democratic American idea is, not that every person shall be made level with every other person, but that every person shall have liberty to be what God made them, without hindrance.

18 *FREDERIC BASTIAT* And what is this liberty, whose very name makes the heart beat faster and shakes the world? Is it not the union of all liberties — liberty of conscience, of education, of association, of the press, of travel, of labor, of trade?

19 *THOMAS JEFFERSON* Rightful liberty is unobstructed action according to our will within the limits drawn around us by the equal rights of others. 20 *THOMAS PAINE* Liberty is the power to do everything that does not interfere with the rights of others. *SCRIBE* Liberty is the defense of a man's right to his property. 21 *JAMES MADISON* For property is that dominion which one man claims and exercises over the external things of the world, in exclusion of every other individual.

A man's land, or merchandise, or money is called his property. In its larger and juster meaning, liberty embraces everything to which a man may attach a value and have a right, and which leaves to everyone else the like advantage. A man has a property in his opinions and the free communication of them; in his religious opinions, and in the profession and practice dictated by them; in the safety and liberty of his person; and in the free use of his faculties and free choice of the objects on which to employ them. In a word, as a man is said to have a right to his property, he may be equally said to have a property in his rights.

22 *JAMES FENIMORE COOPER* Liberty leaves to the citizen freedom of action, and of being. It is the right to pursue happiness in your own manner. Individuality is the aim of political liberty — 23 *RALPH WALDO EMERSON* the significance of the individual; the grandeur of duty; the power of character; being a man of truth, master of his own actions; not in any manner dependent and servile. Forever wells up in man the impulse of choosing and acting in his soul. 24 *ROBERT INGERSOL* What light is to the eyes — what air is to the lungs — what love is to the heart, liberty is to the soul of man.

25 *ALEXANDER HAMILTON* There is a certain enthusiasm in liberty that makes human nature rise above itself, in acts of bravery and heroism. 26 *WILLIAM PITT* This is the glorious spirit of millions in America, who prefer poverty with liberty to gilded chains, and who will die in defense of their rights as men, as free men.

27 *THOMAS JEFFERSON* This was the object of the Declaration of Independence. Not to find out new principles, or new arguments, never before thought of, not merely to say things which had never been said before; but to place before mankind the common sense of the subject, in terms so plain and firm as to command their assent, and to justify ourselves in the independent stand we were compelled to take. It was intended to be an expression of the American mind.

28 *JOHN ADAMS* What do we mean by the American Revolution? Do we mean the American war? The Revolution was affected before the war commenced. The Revolution was in the minds and hearts of the people, a change in their religious sentiments,

of their duties and obligations. This radical change in the principles, opinions, sentiments, and affections of the people was the real American Revolution.

29 *ABRAHAM LINCOLN* It is not the guns of our war steamers, or the strength of our gallant and disciplined army that is the bulwark of our liberty and independence. Not even the Constitution and the Union are the primary cause of our great prosperity, though we could not have done it without these. No, there is something behind all of these, entwining itself more closely about the human heart. That something is the principle of liberty to all — the principle that clears the path for all; gives hope to all; and, by consequence, enterprise and industry to all. It is the preservation of the spirit which prizes liberty as the heritage of all men, in all lands, everywhere.

30 *DECLARATION OF INDEPENDENCE* We hold these truths to be self-evident, that all men are created equal, that they are endowed by their Creator with certain unalienable Rights, that among these are Life, Liberty and the pursuit of Happiness.

31 *JOHN QUINCY ADAMS* The Declaration of Independence was the first solemn declaration, by a nation, of the only legitimate foundation of civil government. It was the cornerstone of a new fabric, destined to cover the surface of the globe. It demolished at a stroke the lawfulness of all governments founded upon conquest. It swept away all the rubbish of accumulated centuries of servitude. It announced in practical form to the world the transcendent truth of the inalienable sovereignty of the people. It stands, and must forever stand, alone — a beacon on the summit of the mountain, to which all the inhabitants of the earth may turn their eyes for a genial and saving light. So long as this planet shall be inhabited by human beings, so long as man shall be of

a social nature, so long as government shall be necessary to the great moral purposes of society, so long as it shall be abused to the purposes of oppression, the Declaration will stand a light of admonition to the rulers of men, a light of salvation and redemption to the oppressed; for it will hold out to the sovereign and to the subject the extent and the boundaries of their respective rights and duties, founded in the laws of nature and of nature's God.

[32] *ABRAHAM LINCOLN* Our fathers brought forth, upon this continent, a new nation, conceived in liberty, and dedicated to the proposition that all men are created equal. [33] *BENJAMIN FRANKLIN* Our cause is the cause of all mankind. [34] *JOHN ADAMS* Our principles of liberty are as universal and unalterable as human nature. [35] *ABRAHAM LINCOLN* Our reliance is not in armies; it is in the love of liberty which God has planted in our hearts. [36] *PHILLIS WHEATLEY* For in every human breast, God has implanted a principle, which we call love of freedom; it is impatient of oppression, and it pants for deliverance.

[37] *W.E.B. DUBOIS* I believe in liberty for all men: the space to stretch your arms and your souls, the right to breathe and the right to vote, the freedom to choose your friends, enjoy the sunshine, and ride on the railroads, uncursed by color, thinking, dreaming, working as you will in a kingdom of beauty and love.

[38] *SAMUEL ADAMS* Just and true liberty — equal and impartial liberty: This is what all men are clearly entitled to by the eternal and immutable laws of God and nature. [39] *BENJAMIN FRANKLIN* And God grant that not only the love of liberty but a thorough knowledge of the rights of man may pervade all the nations of the earth, so that a philosopher may set foot anywhere on its surface and say: "This is my country."

40 *PATRICK HENRY* Liberty, the greatest of all earthly blessings - give us that precious jewel, and you may take everything else. 41 *WILLIAM LLOYD GARRISON* Liberty for each. Liberty for all. Liberty forever.

CHAPTER TWO

CONSCIENCE

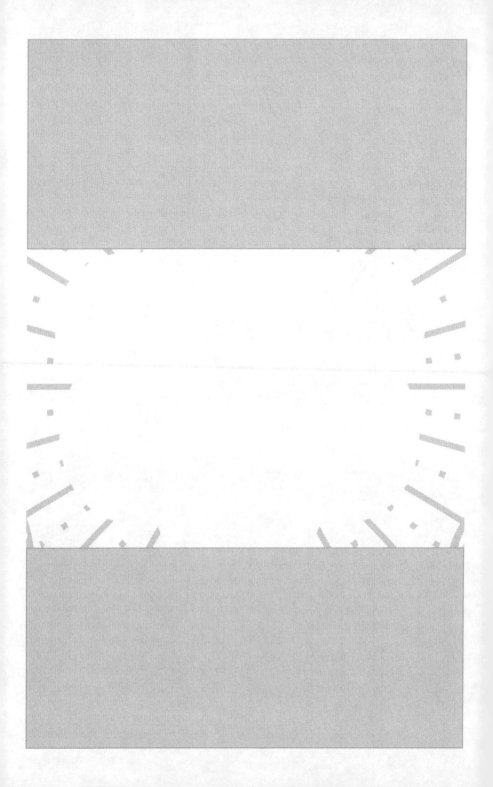

1 *SAMUEL ADAMS* The civil magistrate has everywhere contaminated religion by making it an engine of policy: and freedom of thought and the right of private judgment, in matters of conscience, driven from every other corner of the earth, directed their course to this happy country as their last asylum.

2 *GEORGE WASHINGTON* In this land, the light of truth and reason has triumphed over the power of bigotry and superstition, that every person may here worship God according to the dictates of their own heart; that an individual's religious tenets will not forfeit the protection of the laws; 3 *JAMES MADISON* that religion, or the duty which we owe to our Creator, and the manner of discharging it, can be directed only by reason and conviction, not by force or violence; 4 *GEORGE WASHINGTON* that every man, conducting himself as a good citizen, and being accountable to God alone for his religious opinions, ought to be protected in worshiping the Deity according to the dictates of his own conscience; 5 *JAMES MADISON* that the civil rights of none shall be abridged on account of religious belief or worship, nor shall the full and equal rights of conscience be in any manner, or on any pretext infringed; 6 *THOMAS JEFFERSON* that to compel a man to furnish the contributions of money for the propagation of opinions which he disbelieves and abhors is sinful and tyrannical!

7 *THOMAS JEFFERSON* Our rulers can have authority over our natural rights only as we have submitted to them! The rights of conscience we never submitted — we could not submit! We are answerable for them only to God! 8 *GEORGE WASHINGTON* God alone is the Judge of the hearts of men!

9 *JOHN ADAMS* Let the pulpit resound with the doctrines and sentiments of religious liberty! Let us hear the danger of thralldom[†]

[†]   A state of servitude or submission.

to our consciences from ignorance, extreme poverty, and dependence — in short, from civil and political slavery. Let us see delineated before us, the true map of man — let us hear the dignity of his nature. Let it be known that our liberties are not the grants of princes or parliaments, but original rights, agreed on as maxims and established as preliminaries even before a parliament existed!

10 *JOHN WITHERSPOON* My friends, there is not a single instance in history in which civil liberty was lost and religious liberty preserved entire. If therefore we yield up our temporal property, we at the same time deliver our conscience into bondage. 11 *THOMAS JEFFERSON* Thus no provision in our Constitution ought to be dearer to man than that which protects the rights of conscience against the enterprises of civil authority. 12 *THOMAS JEFFERSON* For Constitutional freedom of religion is the most inalienable and sacred of all human rights. That, 13 *FIRST AMENDMENT TO THE CONSTITUTION (PARTIAL)* Congress shall make no law respecting an establishment of religion or prohibiting the free exercise thereof.

SCRIBE And yet, a paradox, 14 *EDMUND BURKE* for freedom without virtue is not freedom but license to pursue whatever passions prevail in the intemperate mind. 15 *BENJAMIN FRANKLIN* Only a virtuous people are capable of freedom. As nations become corrupt and vicious, they have more need of masters.

16 *EDMUND BURKE* Men are qualified for civil liberty in exact proportion to their disposition to put moral chains on their own appetites; in proportion as their love of justice is above their rapacity; in proportion as their soundness and sobriety of understanding is above their vanity and presumption; and in proportion as they are more disposed to listen to the counsels of the wise and good, in preference to the flattery of knaves. Society cannot exist unless

a controlling power upon will and appetite be placed somewhere, and the less of it there is within, the more there is without. For it is ordained in the eternal constitution of things that men of intemperate minds cannot be free. Their passions forge their chains. [17] *ABRAHAM LINCOLN* And we cannot expect a reversal of human nature, which is God's decree, and can never be reversed.

[18] *JAMES MADISON* Some among us infer that there is not sufficient virtue among men for self-government, and that nothing less than the chains of despotism can restrain them from destroying and devouring one another. [19] *JOHN ADAMS* But I believe human nature itself is evermore an advocate for liberty — that there is in human nature a resentment of injury, an indignation against wrong, a love of truth and a veneration of virtue — that people are capable of understanding, seeing, and feeling the differences between true and false, right and wrong, virtue and vice. These amiable passions are the "latent spark" in each of us. [20] *ABRAHAM LINCOLN* These are the better angels of our nature.

[21] *JAMES MADISON* So I ask, is there no virtue among us? If there be not, we are in a wretched situation. No theoretical checks — no form of government can render us secure. To suppose that any form of government will secure liberty or happiness of a people without any virtue is a chimerical idea. For I operate from this great republican principle, that the people must have virtue and intelligence to select men of virtue and wisdom.

[22] *GEORGE WASHINGTON* And let us with caution indulge the supposition that virtue and morality can be maintained without religion. Whatever may be conceded to the influence of refined education, reason and experience both forbid us to expect that national morality can prevail in exclusion of religious principle. [23] *GEORGE WASHINGTON* Of all the dispositions and habits which lead to

political prosperity, religion and morality are indispensable supports. In vain would that man claim the tribute of patriot who should labor to subvert these great pillars of human happiness, these firmest props of the duties of men and citizens.

24 *GEORGE WASHINGTON* Can it be, that Providence has not connected the permanent felicity of a nation with its virtue? 25 *GEORGE WASHINGTON* Let it simply be asked: Where is the security for property, for reputation, for life, if the sense of religious obligations desert our oaths, which are the instruments of investigation in courts of justice? 26 *THOMAS JEFFERSON* How can the liberties of a nation be thought secure when we have removed their only firm basis, a conviction in the minds of the people that these liberties are a gift of God?

27 *ABRAHAM LINCOLN* We have been preserved these many years in peace and prosperity. We have grown in numbers, wealth, and power, as no other nation has ever grown. But we have forgotten God. We have forgotten the gracious Hand which preserved us in peace, and multiplied and enriched and strengthened us; and we have vainly imagined, in the deceitfulness of our hearts, that all these blessings were produced by some superior wisdom and virtue of our own. Intoxicated with unbroken success, we have become too self-sufficient to feel the necessity of redeeming and preserving grace, too proud to pray to the God that made us. 28 *CHARLES DICKENS* Like some wise men, who, learning to know each planet by its Latin name, we have quite forgotten such small heavenly constellations as charity, forbearance, universal love, and mercy, although these constellations shine by night and day so brightly that the blind may see them; but looking upward at the spangled sky, they see nothing there but the reflection of their own great wisdom and book-learning. People of the world, so busy in thought, turning their eyes towards the

countless spheres that shine above them, reflect only the images their minds contain.

29 *JOHN ADAMS* If a new order of things has commenced, it behooves us to be cautious, that it may not be for the worse. If the abuses of Christianity can be annihilated or diminished, and a more enjoyment of the right of conscience introduced, it will be well; but this will not be accomplished by the abolition of Christianity and the introduction of Grecian mythology, or the worship of modern heroes or heroines, by erecting statues of idolatry to reason or virtue, to beauty or to taste. It is a serious problem to resolve, whether all the abuses of Christianity, even in the darkest ages, when the Pope deposed princes and laid nations under his interdict, were ever so bloody and cruel, ever bore down the independence of the human mind with such terror and intolerance, or taught doctrines which required such implicit credulity to believe, as the present reign of pretended philosophy in France.

30 *EDMUND BURKE* What sort of a thing must be a nation of ferocious and sordid barbarians, destitute of religion, honor, or manly pride, possessing nothing at present, and hoping for nothing hereafter? Their liberty is not liberal. Their science is presumptuous ignorance. Their humanity is savage and brutal. 31 *JOHN ADAMS* Hence, they could never be governed but by force since neither virtue, prudence, wisdom, nor anything else sufficed to restrain their passions.

32 *EDMUND BURKE* True religion is the foundation of society. When that is once shaken by contempt, the whole fabric can be neither stable nor lasting. 33 *NOAH WEBSTER* And all the miseries and evils which men suffer from; vice, crime, ambition, injustice, oppression, slavery and war, precede from their despising or neglecting the precepts contained in the Bible.

34 THOMAS JEFFERSON To the corruptions of Christianity I am opposed; but not to the genuine precepts of Jesus himself. I am a Christian in the sense in which he wished any one to be; sincerely attached to his doctrines in preference to all others. *35 JOHN ADAMS* For I have examined all religions as well as my narrow sphere, my straightened means, and my busy life would allow; and the result is that the Bible is the best book in the world. It contains more philosophy than all the libraries I have seen.

36 JOHN ADAMS Suppose a nation of people in some distant region should regulate their conduct by the precepts of the Bible. Every member would be obliged in conscience, to temperance, frugality, and industry; to justice, kindness, and charity toward his fellow men; and to piety, love, and reverence toward Almighty God. What a utopia! What a paradise, would this region be!

SCRIBE But when the people neglect the precepts of the Bible, *37 DANIEL WEBSTER* when the public mind becomes vitiated and corrupt, laws are a nullity and constitutions are but wastepaper. *38 BENJAMIN FRANKLIN* And when the people become corrupted, they will need a despotic government, being incapable of any other.

39 JOHN ADAMS We have no government armed with power capable of contending with human passions unbridled by morality and religion. Corruption, revenge, ambition, or envy will break the strongest cords of our Constitution as a whale goes through a net. Our Constitution was made only for a moral and religious people. It is wholly inadequate to the government of any other. *40 SAMUEL ADAMS* For a general dissolution of principles and manners will more surely overthrow the liberties of America than the whole force of a common enemy!

41 JOHN ADAMS My fellow citizens, the only foundation of a free

Constitution is pure virtue, and if this cannot be inspired into the people in a greater measure than they have it now, then we may change our rulers and the forms of government, but we will not obtain a lasting liberty! 42 *SAMUEL ADAMS* For once the people lose their virtue, they will be ready to surrender their liberties to the first external or internal invader. Our liberty will not long survive the total extinction of morals!

43 *PATRICK HENRY* Reader! Whoever you are, remember this, and in your sphere, practice virtue yourself and encourage it in others. 44 *GEORGE WASHINGTON* Labor to keep alive in your breast that little spark of celestial fire called conscience. 45 *PHILIPPIANS 4:8* Whatever is true, whatever is honorable, whatever is just, whatever is pure, whatever is lovely, whatever is commendable, if there is any excellence, if there is anything worthy of praise, think about these things.

46 *TECUMSEH* When you rise in the morning, give thanks for the light, for your life, for your strength. Give thanks for your food and for the joy of living. If you see no reason to give thanks, the fault lies in yourself.

47 *THOMAS JEFFERSON* Set a resolution, not to be shaken, never to tell an untruth. For falsehood of the tongue leads to that of the heart, and in time depraves all its good dispositions. 48 *PROVERBS 4:23* And above all else, guard your heart, for everything you do flows from it.

49 *ABIGAIL ADAMS* To be good, to do good — this is the whole duty of mankind comprised in a few words. 50 *MICAH 6:8* And He has shown you, O man, what is good. And what does the LORD require of you but to do justly; to love mercy; and to walk humbly with your God; 51 *MATTHEW 5:16* to let your light shine before men; 52 *THOMAS JEFFERSON* to love your neighbor as yourself,

and your country more than yourself; [53] *IMMANUEL KANT* to live your life as though your every act were to become a universal law; [54] *BENJAMIN FRANKLIN* to give to your enemy, forgiveness; to an opponent, tolerance; to a friend, your heart; to your child, a good example; to a father, deference; to your mother, conduct that will make her proud of you; to yourself, respect; to all, grace and charity; [55] *GEORGE WASHINGTON* to entertain a brotherly affection and love for one another, for your fellow citizens of the United States at large, and particularly for your brethren who have served in the field, and finally, that He would most graciously be pleased to dispose us all to demean ourselves with that charity, humility, and pacifying temper of mind which were the characteristics of the Divine Author of our blessed religion, and without a humble imitation of whose example in these things, we can never hope to be a happy nation.

SCRIBE A French diplomat traveled to America, and upon his return, wrote: [56] *ALEXIS DE TOCQUEVILLE* I sought for the greatness and genius of America in her commodious harbors and her ample rivers, and it was not there; in her fertile fields and boundless forests, and it was not there; in her rich mines and her vast world commerce, and it was not there; in her public school system and her institutions of learning, and it was not there; in her democratic Congress and her matchless Constitution, and it was not there. Not until I went into the churches of America and heard her pulpits flame with righteousness did I understand the secret of her genius and power. America is great because she is good, and if America ever ceases to be good, she will cease to be great.

CHAPTER THREE

AGENCY

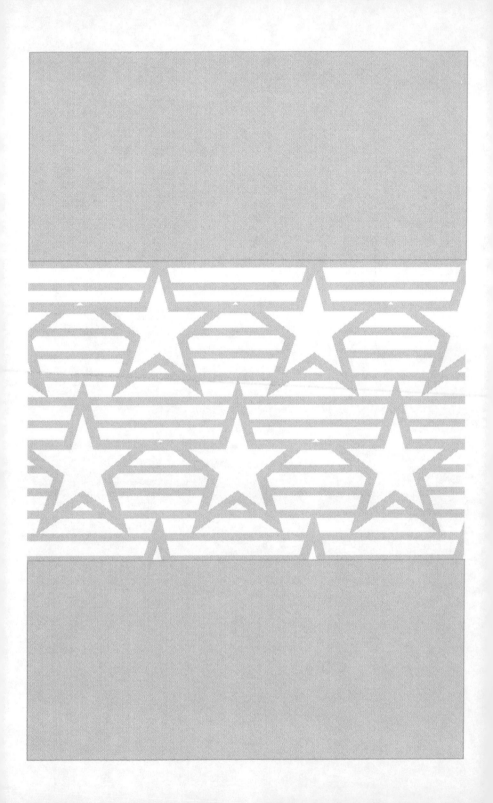

1 THOMAS PAINE When I contemplate the natural dignity of humanity, the honor and happiness of its character, I become irate at the attempt to govern mankind by force and fraud, as if we were all knaves and fools.

2 ALEXIS DE TOCQUEVILLE In these systems, government stands above men as an immense and tutelary power, which takes upon itself alone to secure their gratifications, and to watch over their fate. That power is absolute, minute, regular, provident, and mild. It would be like the authority of a parent if, like that authority, its object was to prepare men for manhood; but it seeks, on the contrary, to keep them in perpetual childhood. For their happiness such a government willingly labors, but it chooses to be the sole agent and the only arbiter of that happiness; it provides for their security, foresees and supplies their necessities, facilitates their pleasures, manages their principal concerns, directs their industry, regulates their property, and subdivides their inheritances.

After having thus successively taken each member of the community in its powerful grasp and fashioned him at will, the supreme power then extends its arm over the whole community. It covers the surface of society with a network of small complicated rules, minute and uniform, through which the most original minds and the most energetic characters cannot penetrate, to rise above the crowd. The will of man is not shattered, but softened, bent, and guided; men are seldom forced by it to act, but they are constantly restrained from acting. Such a power does not destroy, but it prevents existence; it does not tyrannize, but it compresses, enervates, extinguishes, and stupefies a people, till each nation is reduced to nothing better than a flock of timid and industrious animals, of which the government is the shepherd.

3 FREDERIC BASTIAT They would be the shepherds over us, their sheep.

4 *ALEXIS DE TOCQUEVILLE* What remains, but to spare us the care of thinking and all the trouble of living?

5 *ALEXIS DE TOCQUEVILLE* A nation cannot long remain strong when every person belonging to it is individually weak. No form or combination of social polity has yet been devised to make an energetic people out of a community of pusillanimous[†] and enfeebled citizens.

6 *THOMAS JEFFERSON* Mankind, by its constitution, is naturally divided into two parties: Those who fear and distrust the people and wish to draw all powers from them into the hands of the elite. And those who identify themselves with the people, have confidence in them, cherish and consider them as most honest and trustworthy. In every country these two parties exist; and in every one where people are free to think, speak, and write, these two parties will declare themselves. *SCRIBE* And so we shall.

7 *DANIEL WEBSTER* Instead of dwelling in those caverns of darkness, instead of groping with those ideas so full of all that is horrid and horrible, we come out into the light of day; we enjoy the fresh air of liberty and union; we cherish those hopes which belong to us; we devote ourselves to those great objects that are fit for our consideration and our action. 8 *DANIEL WEBSTER* Our aspirations are as high as our country's certain destiny; our daily respiration is liberty and patriotism; our veins are full of enterprise, courage, and honor.

9 *JOHN JAY* We believe that the people are truly the sovereigns of the country, but they are sovereigns without subjects — with none to govern but themselves; that citizens of America are equal as

---

†   Timid.

fellow citizens, and as joint tenants in their sovereignty.

10 *GEORGE WASHINGTON* We believe that a freeman, contending for liberty on his own ground, is superior to any slavish mercenary on earth; 11 *JAMES WILSON* that a man is capable of managing his own affairs and answerable for his conduct toward others; 12 *JOHN LOCKE* that the most precious of all our possessions is power over ourselves.

13 *SCRIBE* We believe that gratitude bestows reverence, changing forever how we experience life and the world; 14 *HENRY WARD BEECHER* that a thankful heart will find, in every hour, some heavenly blessings.

15 *GEORGE WASHINGTON* We believe that human happiness and moral duty are inseparably connected; that your love of liberty — your respect for the laws — your habits of industry — your practice of the moral and religious obligations, these are our strongest claims to national and individual happiness.

16 *THOMAS JEFFERSON* Our greatest happiness does not depend on the condition of life in which chance has placed us. 17 *SCRIBE* We do not complain because rose bushes have thorns; we rejoice because thorn bushes have roses! 18 *GEORGE WASHINGTON* For we know that happiness depends more upon the internal frame of a person's own mind than on the externals of this world.

19 *THOMAS JEFFERSON* The happiest moments of our lives are those passed at home in the bosom of our family, 20 *ABIGAIL ADAMS* seeing our family again collected under our own roof, happy in ourselves, and blessed in each other.

21 *THOMAS JEFFERSON* For me, I had rather be shut up in a very modest cottage, with my books, my family, and a few old friends, dining

on simple bacon, and letting the world roll on as it liked, than to occupy the most splendid post which any human power can give. [22] *BENJAMIN FRANKLIN* For it is the man and woman united that makes the complete human being, and therefore the state in which you are most likely to find solid happiness. Together they are more likely to succeed in the world. For man has not nearly the value he would have in the state of union. He is an incomplete animal; he resembles the odd half of a pair of scissors.

[23] *THOMAS JEFFERSON* My friends, it is in the love of one's family only that heartfelt happiness is known. *SCRIBE* And when our families join together in faith, [24] *JOHN WINTHROP* we have before our eyes, our commission and community as members of the same body. [25] *JOHN WINTHROP* We knit together as one; we entertain each other in brotherly affection; we uphold a familiar commerce together in all meekness, gentleness, patience, and liberality; we delight in each other, make others' conditions our own, rejoice together, mourn together, labor, and suffer together, always having before our eyes our commission and community as members of the same body. [26] *GEORGE WASHINGTON* We let our heart feel for the afflictions and distresses of everyone, and let our hand give in proportion to our purse, [27] *JOHN WINTHROP* willingly abridging ourselves of our supply, for the supply of others. [28] *GALATIANS 3:28* For there is neither Jew nor Greek; there is neither slave nor free man; there is neither male nor female; for all are one in Christ Jesus.

SCRIBE In describing the exceptional nature of the American people, the French diplomat observed: [29] *ALEXIS DE TOCQUEVILLE* I must say that I have often seen Americans make great and real sacrifices to the public welfare; and I have noticed a hundred instances in which they hardly ever failed to lend faithful support to one another. The free institutions which the inhabitants of the United States possess, and the political rights of which they make so much use, remind every citizen, and in a thousand ways, that they live in a society. They every instant impress upon a person's mind the notion that it is the duty as well as the interest of every citizen to make themselves useful to their fellow creatures. Their hearts thus readily lean to the side of kindness. For people attend to the interests of the public, first by necessity, afterwards by choice; what was intentional becomes an instinct, and by dint of working for the good of one's fellow citizens, the habit and the taste for serving them are at length acquired.

30 *ALEXIS DE TOCQUEVILLE* Americans create associations of a thousand kinds, religious, moral, serious, futile, general or restricted, enormous or diminutive: associations to give entertainments, to found seminaries, to build inns, to construct churches, to diffuse books, to send missionaries to the antipodes; in this manner they found hospitals, prisons, and schools; each proposed to inculcate some truth, or to foster some feeling by the encouragement of a great example. And in so doing, they form a society. Wherever at the head of some new undertaking you see the government in France, or a man of rank in England, in the United States you will be sure to find an association of private citizens.

31 *ALEXIS DE TOCQUEVILLE* In any community in this country, a citizen may conceive of some need that is not being met. What does the citizen do? They go across the street and discuss it with their neighbor. Then what happens? A committee begins functioning on behalf of that need. All of this is done by individuals on their own initiative.

32 *SCRIBE* Do you want to know how you can help your country? Don't ask. Act! It is action that delineates and defines you. 33 *PHILIPPIANS 2:4* Not looking to your private good, but keeping in

mind the good of others. *SCRIBE* To find that mission you can give yourself over to, and then to spend your days moving that mission forward. You are made so that when anything fires your soul the impossibilities vanish!

34 *THEODORE ROOSEVELT* It is not the critic who counts; not the man who points out how the strong man stumbles, or where the doer of deeds could have done them better. The credit belongs to the man who is actually in the arena, whose face is marred by dust and sweat and blood; who strives to do the deeds; who knows great enthusiasms, the great devotions; who spends himself in a worthy cause; who at the best knows in the end the triumph of high achievement, and who at the worst, if he fails, at least fails while daring greatly, so that his place shall never be with those cold and timid souls who neither know victory nor defeat.

35 *JOHN QUINCY ADAMS* My fellow citizens, your individual liberty is your individual power, and as the power of a community is a mass compounded of powerful individuals, the nation whose people enjoys the most freedom will be, in proportion to its numbers, the most powerful nation on earth! 36 *SCRIBE* For we do not rest our political experiments upon the power of government. Far from it, 37 *JAMES MADISON* we rest all our political experiments on the capacity of mankind for self-government.

38 *JOHN ADAMS* A Constitution founded on these principles introduces knowledge among the people and inspires them with a conscious dignity becoming freemen; a general emulation takes place, which causes good humor, sociability, good manners, and good morals to be general. That elevation of sentiment inspired by such a government makes men brave and enterprising. That ambition, which is inspired by it, makes them sober, industrious, and frugal.

[39] *THOMAS JEFFERSON* What inheritance so valuable can man leave to his posterity as this? That men may be trusted to govern themselves without a master; [40] *ALEXIS DE TOCQUEVILLE* that the health of a nation, of a democratic society, may be measured by the quality of functions performed by private citizens; [41] *THOMAS JEFFERSON* that our Declaration of Independence may be to the world the signal arousing men to burst the chains under which monkish ignorance and superstition had persuaded them to bind themselves, and to assume the blessings and security of self-government.

CHAPTER FOUR

KNOWLEDGE

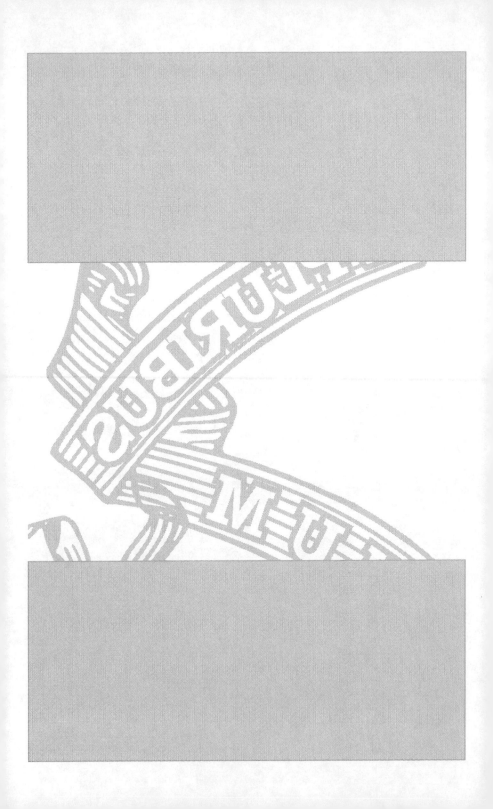

1 *JOHN ADAMS* Without wishing to damp the ardor of curiosity or influence the freedom of inquiry, I will hazard a prediction that, after the most industrious and impartial researches, the longest liver of you will find no principles, institutions, or systems of education more fit in general to be transmitted to your posterity than those you have received from your ancestors. *SCRIBE* Let us, therefore, consider the Founders' forebears.

2 *JOHN ADAMS* The early Adventurers, so often mentioned, had an utter contempt of all hereditary indefeasible† right — the Lord's anointed — and the divine miraculous original of government, with which the priesthood had enveloped the feudal monarch in clouds and mysteries. They knew that government was a plain, simple, intelligible thing founded in nature and reason and quite comprehensible by common sense. They detested all the base services and servile dependencies of the feudal system. They knew that no such unworthy dependences took place in the ancient seats of liberty, the Republic of Greece and Rome. They thought all such slavish subordinations were equally inconsistent with the constitution of human nature and that religious liberty, with which Jesus had made them free.

They saw clearly that popular powers must be placed as a guard, a control, a balance, to the powers of the monarch and the priest in every government, or else it would soon become a great and detestable system of fraud, violence, and usurpation. Their greatest concern seems to have been to establish a government of the church more consistent with the scriptures, and a government of the state more agreeable to the dignity of human nature, than any they had seen in Europe — and to transmit

---

† Not able to be undone, voided, or overturned.

such a government down to their posterity, with the means of securing and preserving it, forever.

3 *THOMAS JEFFERSON* History, by apprising us of the past, enables us to judge the future; it avails us of the experience of other times and other nations; it qualifies us as judges of the actions and designs of men; and it enables us to know ambition under every disguise it may assume — and knowing it, to defeat its views.

4 *JOHN JAY* I consider knowledge to be the soul of a republic. 5 *GEORGE WASHINGTON* For to the security of a free Constitution, knowledge contributes by teaching the people themselves to know and to value their own rights, to discern and provide against invasions of them, to distinguish between oppression and the necessary exercise of lawful authority. 6 *JOHN JAY* For as the weak and the wicked are generally in alliance, much care should be taken to diminish the number of the former as of the latter.

7 *ALEXANDER HAMILTON* The safety of a republic depends essentially on the energy of a common national sentiment; on a uniformity of principles and habits; on the exemptions of the citizens from foreign bias and prejudice; and on a love of country which will almost invariably be found to be closely connected with birth, education and family. 8 *GEORGE WASHINGTON* For you are citizens, by birth or choice, of a common country, and that country has a right to concentrate your affections.

The name of **AMERICAN**, which belongs to you, in your national capacity, must always exalt the just pride of patriotism, more than any appellation derived from local discriminations. For with slight shades of difference, you have the same religion, manners, habits & political principles. You have in a common cause fought and triumphed together—the independence and liberty you possess are the work of joint councils, and joint efforts—of common dangers, sufferings and successes.

9 *HENRY WARD BEECHER* When I see a nation's flag, I see not the flag only, but the nation itself; the government, the principles, the truths, the history which belongs to the nation that sets it forth. 10 *HENRY WARD BEECHER* If anyone asks me the meaning of our flag, I say to him — it means just what Concord and Lexington meant; what Bunker Hill meant: which was, in short, the rising up of a valiant, young people against an old tyranny to establish the most momentous doctrine that the world has ever known — the right of individuals to their own selves and to their liberties.

11 *THOMAS JEFFERSON* I know no safe depository of the ultimate powers of the society but the people themselves; and if we think them not enlightened enough to exercise their control with a wholesome discretion, the remedy is not to take it from them but to inform their discretion by education. 12 *BENJAMIN RUSH* For without learning, men are incapable of knowing their rights, and where learning is confined to a few people, liberty can be neither equal nor universal.

13 *JAMES MONROE* It is only when the people become ignorant and corrupt, when they degenerate into a populace, that they are incapable of exercising their sovereignty. Usurpation is then an easy attainment, and a usurper soon found. The people themselves become the willing instruments of their own debasement and ruin.

SCRIBE To those who would usurp the sovereignty of the people, 14 *ALEXANDER HAMILTON* the fundamental source of all your errors, sophisms, and false reasonings, is a total ignorance of the natural rights of mankind. Were you once to become acquainted with these, you could never entertain a thought, that all men are not, by nature, entitled to a parity of privileges. You would be convinced, that natural liberty is a gift of the beneficent Creator, to the whole human race; and that civil liberty is founded in that; and cannot be wrested from any people without the most manifest violation of justice. For civil liberty is only natural liberty, not a thing dependent on human will and caprice; but is innate and agreeable to the constitution of man, as well as necessary to the well-being of society.

15 *JAMES MADISON* If we the people mean to be our own governors; we must arm ourselves with the power which knowledge gives. 16 *JOHN ADAMS* Let us, therefore, tenderly and kindly cherish the means of knowledge. Let us dare to read, think, speak, and write. Let us become attentive to the grounds and principles of government. Let us study the law of nature; search into the spirit of the Constitution; read the histories of ancient ages; contemplate the great examples of Greece and Rome, and study our great ancestors who have defended for us the inherent rights of mankind against foreign and domestic tyrants and usurpers; against arbitrary kings and cruel priests; in short, against the gates of earth and hell. Let us examine into the nature of that power and the cruelty of that oppression which drove the Adventurers from their homes. Recollect their amazing fortitude, their bitter sufferings! The hunger, the nakedness, the cold, which they patiently endured! Let us recollect the civil and religious principles and hopes and expectations which constantly supported and carried them through all hardships, and patience and resignation! Let us recollect it was liberty! The hope of liberty for themselves and us and ours, which conquered all discouragements, dangers, and trials! In such researches as these let us all cheerfully engage as proper patrons and supporters of law, learning, and religion.

Let us be informed of the mighty struggles and numberless

sacrifices made by our ancestors in defense of freedom. Let us search for the foundations of laws and government in the frame of human nature, in the constitution of the intellectual and moral world. There let us see that truth, liberty, justice, and benevolence, are its everlasting basis. Let the colleges join their harmony in the same delightful concern.

Let every declamation turn upon the beauty of liberty and virtue, and the deformity, turpitude†, and malignity of slavery and vice. Let us research the grounds and nature and ends of government, and the means of preserving the good and demolishing the evil. Let the dialogues and all the exercises become the instruments of impressing on the tender mind, and of spreading and distributing, far and wide, the ideas of right and the sensations of freedom.

17 *JOHN ADAMS* My friends, I study politics and war, that my children may have liberty to study mathematics and philosophy. My children study mathematics and philosophy, geography, natural history and naval architecture, navigation, commerce, and agriculture in order to give their children a right to study painting, poetry, music, architecture, statuary, tapestry, and porcelain.

18 *BENJAMIN FRANKLIN* Truth be told, the rapid progress of the sciences makes me regret sometimes that I was born so soon. For it is impossible to imagine the height to which it may be carried in a thousand years through the power of man over matter. O, that moral sciences were in as far a way of improvement, that men would cease to be wolves to one another, and that human beings would at length learn what they now improperly call humanity.

---

† Wickedness.

19 BENJAMIN FRANKLIN At my father's table he liked to have, as often as he could, some sensible friend or neighbor to converse with, and always took care to start some ingenious or useful topic for discourse which might tend to improve the minds of his children. By this means he turned our attention to what was good, just, and prudent in the conduct of life.

20 JOHN ADAMS It should be your care, therefore, and mine, to elevate the minds of our children and exalt their courage; to accelerate and animate their industry and activity; to excite in them a habitual contempt of meanness, abhorrence of injustice and inhumanity, and ambition to excel in every capacity, faculty, and virtue. If we suffer their minds to grovel and creep in infancy, they will grovel all their lives.

21 NOAH WEBSTER Every child in America should be acquainted with their own country. Children should read books that furnish them with ideas that will be useful to them in life and practice. As soon as they open their lips, they should rehearse the history of their own country. They should lisp the praise of liberty, and of those illustrious heroes and statesmen who have wrought a revolution in her favor: they should read essays on the settlement and geography of America; they should know the history of the late Revolution and of the most remarkable characters and events that distinguished it, and the principles of the federal and state governments. Systems of education should be adopted and pursued which may not only diffuse a knowledge of the sciences but may implant in the minds of the American youth the principles of virtue and of liberty and inspire them with just and liberal ideas of government and with an inviolable attachment to their country.

22 SAMUEL ADAMS Such an education will enlarge their powers of mind, and prompt them impartially to search for truth in the consideration of every subject that may employ their thoughts. *23 JAMES MADISON* For we must be cultivators of the human mind, the manufacturers of useful knowledge, the agents of the commerce of ideas, the teachers of the arts of life, *24 JAMES FENIMORE COOPER* the lovers of truth — not the mere love of facts expressed by true names and dates, but the love of that higher truth, the truth of nature and principals.

25 ABIGAIL ADAMS My friends, learning is not attained by chance; it must be sought for with ardor and attended to with diligence. *26 THOMAS JEFFERSON* Be bold in the pursuit of knowledge! *27 IMMANUEL KANT* Sapere aude! Dare to know! Have the courage to use your own intelligence. *28 FRANCIS BACON* Seek the knowledge of causes, the bounds of human empire, and the effecting of all things possible. *29 RALPH WALDO EMERSON* Explore, and explore, and explore! *30 FREDERICK DOUGLASS* For education means emancipation! It means light and liberty! It means the uplifting of the soul of man into the glorious light of truth, the light by which men can only be made free!

31 THOMAS JEFFERSON My fellow citizens, if any nation expects to be ignorant and free, in a state of civilization, it expects what never was, and never will be.

SPEECH

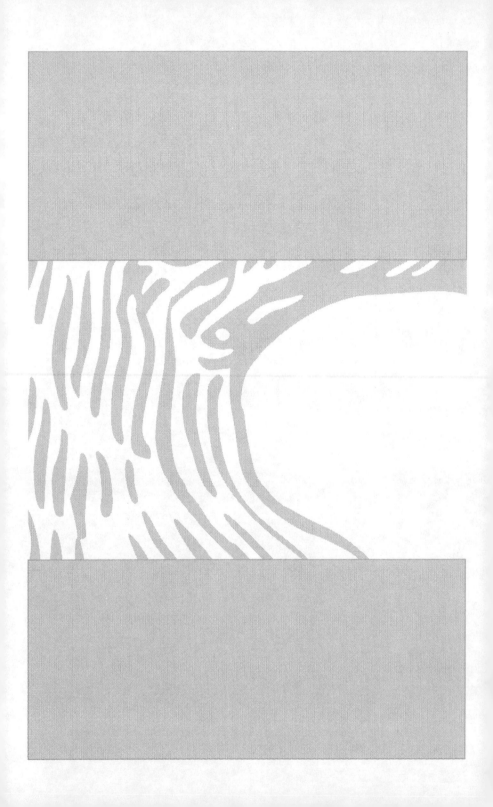

1 JOHN ADAMS In the earliest ages of the world, absolute monarchy seems to have been the universal form of government. Kings exercised a cruel tyranny over the people. *2 THOMAS PAINE* Hither have they fled, not from the tender embraces of the mother, but from the cruelty of the monster.

3 THOMAS PAINE O, ye that love mankind! Ye that dare oppose, not only the tyranny, but the tyrant, stand forth! Every spot of the old world is overrun with oppression. Freedom hath been hunted round the globe. Asia, and Africa, have long expelled her. Europe regards her like a stranger, and England hath given her warning to depart. *4 THOMAS PAINE* O! Receive the fugitive and prepare in time an asylum for mankind.

SCRIBE And an asylum they created. For in the United States, *5 JAMES MADISON* the First Amendment protects our right to think what we like and say what we please. And if we the people are to govern ourselves, we must have these rights, even if they are misused by a minority.

6 BENJAMIN FRANKLIN Freedom of speech is a principal pillar of a free government. It is the right of every human being, as far as it does not hurt the right of another; this is the only check it ought to suffer and the only bounds it ought to know. *7 HENRY WARD BEECHER* For there is tonic in the things that men do not love to hear. Free speech is to a great people what the winds are to oceans, and where free speech is stopped, miasma† is bred, and death comes fast.

8 BENJAMIN FRANKLIN Printers are educated in the belief, that when men differ in opinion, both sides ought equally to have the advantage of being heard by the public. For when truth and error have fair

---

† Vaporous emanation formerly believed to cause disease.

play, the former is always an overmatch for the latter. *SCRIBE* But only when truth and error have fair play. [9] *JOHN STUART MILL* For the dictum that truth always triumphs over persecution is one of those pleasant falsehoods that men repeat after one another until they become common knowledge, but which all experience refutes. History teems with instances of truth put down by persecution. Even if not suppressed forever, it can be thrown back for centuries.

[10] *JOHN STUART MILL* Unfortunately, the fact that people are fallible does not carry nearly as much weight in practice as it is allowed to carry in theory. Everyone knows perfectly well they are fallible, but few think it necessary to take any precautions against their own fallibility. [11] *THOMAS JEFFERSON* Hence, they attempt to influence free speech by temporal punishments, or burdens, or by civil incapacitations, [12] *JOHN LOCKE* or by censuring a man who follows his own thoughts in the search of truth, when it leads him ever so little out of the common road.

[13] *JOHN STUART MILL* The peculiar evil of silencing the expression of an opinion is that it is robbing not one individual but the human race; those who dissent from the opinion even more than those who hold it. If the opinion is right, the dissenter is deprived of the opportunity of exchanging error for truth. If the opinion is wrong, the dissenter loses the clearer perception and livelier impression of truth, produced by its collision with error. [14] *JOHN STUART MILL* For he who knows only his own side of the argument knows little of that. His reasons may be good, and no one may have been able to refute them. But if he is equally unable to refute the reasons on the opposite side, if he does not so much as know what they are, he has no ground for preferring either opinion.

[15] *JOHN STUART MILL* Cicero, the ancient orator, has left it on record

that he always studied his adversary's case as intensely as he did his own, if not even more so. What Cicero practiced as the means of success in the law courts should be imitated by anyone who studies any subject in order to arrive at the truth. It isn't enough that he should hear the arguments of opponents from his own teachers, presented in their way and accompanied by what they offer as refutations. That isn't the way to do justice to the opposing arguments, or to bring them into real contact with his own mind. He must be able to hear them from people who actually believe them, defend them in earnest, and do their very best for them. If he doesn't know the opposing arguments in their most plausible and persuasive form, he will never really possess the portion of truth.

16 *JOHN STUART MILL* The absence of discussion leads men to forget not only the grounds for an opinion but too often also its meaning. The words in which it is expressed cease to suggest ideas or suggest only a small portion of the ideas they were originally used to communicate. Instead of a vivid conception and a living belief, there remain only a few phrases learned by heart; or if any part of the meaning is retained it is only the shell and husk of it, the finer essence being lost.

17 *JOHN STUART MILL* There are people who will be satisfied if you assent undoubtingly to something that they think is true. And when such people get their creed to be taught as authoritative, they naturally think that no good and some harm will come from allowing it to be questioned. 18 *ALEXIS DE TOCQUEVILLE* As when a large number of organs of the press come to advance along the same track, their influence becomes almost irresistible in the long term, and public opinion, struck always from the same side, ends by yielding under their blows. 19 *JOHN STUART MILL* And where

their influence is dominant, they make it nearly impossible for the publicly-accepted opinion to be rejected wisely and considerately. They have a belief that owes nothing to argument and isn't vulnerable to argument — this isn't the way truth ought to be held by a rational being. This is not knowing the truth. Truth when accepted in this way is merely one more superstition.

[20] *JOHN STUART MILL* Of course those who want to suppress speech will deny its truth; but they aren't infallible. They have no authority to decide the question for all mankind and exclude every other person from the means of judging. To refuse a hearing of an opinion because they are sure that it is false is to assume that their certainty is the same thing as absolute certainty.

[21] *JOHN STUART MILL* I deny the right of the people to exercise such coercion, whether directly or through their government. The power of coercion itself is illegitimate. The best government has no more right to it than the worst.

[22] *GEORGE WASHINGTON* If we are to be precluded from offering sentiments on a matter, which may involve the most serious and alarming consequences that can invite the consideration of mankind, then reason is of no use to us; the freedom of speech may be taken away, and dumb and silent we may be led, like sheep to the slaughter! [23] *BENJAMIN FRANKLIN* For without freedom of thought, there can be no such thing as wisdom. And no such thing as liberty without freedom of speech! [24] *ROBERT INGERSOLL* And without liberty, the brain is a dungeon, where chained thoughts die!

[25] *THOMAS PAINE* All who would make their own liberty secure, must guard even their enemy from oppression; for if you violate this duty, you establish a precedent that will reach yourself. [26] *JOHN STUART MILL* If all mankind minus one were of one opinion,

mankind would be no more justified in silencing that one person than he, if he had the power, would be justified in silencing them if he could.

27 *THOMAS JEFFERSON* If there be any among us who would wish to dissolve this union or to change its republican form, let them stand undisturbed as monuments of the safety with which error of opinion may be tolerated where reason is left free to combat it. 28 *JOHN ADAMS* For facts are stubborn things; and whatever may be your wishes, inclinations, or the dictates of your passions, they cannot alter the state of facts and evidence. 29 *THOMAS JEFFERSON* Thus we are not afraid to follow truth wherever it may lead, nor afraid to tolerate any error, where reason is left free to combat it.

SCRIBE This includes the press. 30 *THOMAS JEFFERSON* Our liberty depends on the freedom of the press, and that cannot be limited without being lost. 31 *JAMES MADISON* For to the press alone, checkered as it is with abuses, the world is indebted for all the triumphs which have been gained by reason and humanity over error and oppression. 32 *THOMAS JEFFERSON* The press needs no other legal restraint; public judgment will correct false reasonings and opinions, on a full hearing of all parties; and no other definite line can be drawn between the inestimable liberty of the press and its demoralizing licentiousness.

33 *THOMAS JEFFERSON* Sadly, nothing can now be believed which is seen in a newspaper. Truth itself becomes suspicious by being put into that polluted vehicle. The real extent of this state of misinformation is known only to those who are in situations to confront facts within their knowledge with the lies of the day. I really look with commiseration over the great body of my fellow citizens, who, reading newspapers, live and die in the belief, that they have known something of what has been passing in the world in their time;

whereas the accounts they have read in newspapers are fiction, except that the real names of the day are affixed to their fables.

34 *THOMAS JEFFERSON* During this administration, and in order to disturb it, the artillery of the press has been leveled against us, charged with whatsoever its licentiousness could devise or dare. 35 *THOMAS JEFFERSON* We became the butt of everything which reason, ridicule, malice, and falsehood can supply. They have concentrated all their hatred on us till they have really persuaded themselves that we are the sole source of all their imaginary evils.

SCRIBE But we will not be silenced by our adversaries, nor intimidated by the press, 36 *ABRAHAM LINCOLN* nor slandered from our duty by false accusations, nor frightened from it by threats of destruction. We have faith that right makes might and in that faith, let us to the end, dare to do our duty!

37 *THOMAS JEFFERSON* To preserve the freedom of the human mind, every spirit should be ready to devote itself to martyrdom! 38 *JOHN ADAMS* For the jaws of power are always open to devour, and her arms are always stretched out, if possible, to destroy the freedom of thinking, speaking, and writing!

SCRIBE As I stand here before you, 39 *THOMAS JEFFERSON* I have sworn upon the altar of God eternal hostility against every form of tyranny over the mind of man! 40 *BENJAMIN FRANKLIN* For whoever would overthrow the liberty of a nation, will begin by subduing the freeness of speech!

41 *BENJAMIN FRANKLIN* Citizens! Freedom of speech IS the great bulwark of liberty; they prosper and die together!

42 *PATRICK HENRY* If we wish to be free, if we mean to preserve inviolate the liberty for which we have been so long contending, we must

fight! [43] *THOMAS JEFFERSON* To think as we will. To speak as we think. To prove that mankind can be governed by reason: that the condition of man can proceed in improvement; [44] *GEORGE WASHINGTON* that intellectual light can spring up in the dark corners of the earth; that freedom of inquiry can produce liberality of conduct; and that mankind can reverse the absurd position that the many were made for the few!

[45] *JAMES MADISON* The unconstitutional power exercised over the press, and the free communication among the people, ought to produce universal alarm. For freedom of speech has ever been justly deemed the only effectual guardian of every other right. Thus, [46] *FIRST AMENDMENT TO THE CONSTITUTION* Congress shall make no law respecting an establishment of religion, or prohibiting the free exercise thereof; or abridging the freedom of speech, or of the press; or the right of the people peaceably to assemble, and to petition the Government for a redress of grievances.

[47] *THOMAS JEFFERSON* No experiment can be more interesting than that we are now trying, and which we trust will end in establishing the fact that man may be governed by reason and truth. Our first object should therefore be to leave open to him all the avenues to truth. [48] *THOMAS PAINE* For it is the irresistible nature of truth, that all it asks, and all it wants, is the liberty of appearing.

CHAPTER SIX

CONSTITUTION

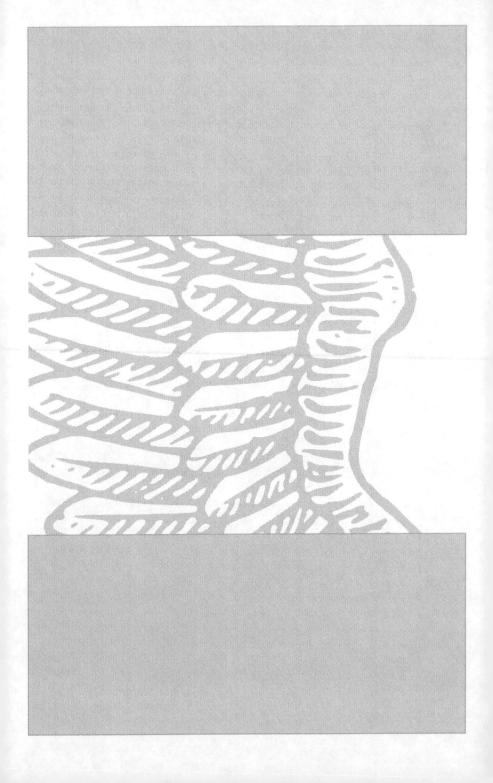

1 *ALEXANDER HAMILTON* The sacred rights of mankind are not to be rummaged for among old parchments or musty records. They are written, as with a sunbeam, in the whole volume of human nature, by the Hand of the Divinity, and can never be erased. 2 *ALEXANDER HAMILTON* So why has government been instituted at all? Because the passions of men will not conform to the dictates of reason and justice without constraint. 3 *THOMAS HOBBES* Simply said, the passions of men are commonly more potent than their reason. 4 *GEORGE WASHINGTON* And we must take human nature as we find it, for perfection falls not to the share of mortals. 5 *JAMES MADISON* For what is government itself, but the greatest of all reflections on human nature?

6 *JAMES MADISON* If men were angels, no government would be necessary. If angels were to govern men, neither external nor internal controls on government would be necessary. In framing a government which is to be administered by men over men, the great difficulty lies in this: you must first enable the government to control the governed; and in the next place, oblige it to control itself. 7 *THOMAS JEFFERSON* For man is not made for the state, but the state for man, and it derives its just powers from the consent of the governed — 8 *DANIEL WEBSTER* the people's government, made for the people, made by the people, and answerable to the people.

9 *JAMES MADISON* In Europe, charters of liberty have been granted by power. But America has set the example of charters of power granted by liberty. This revolution in the practice of the world may, with an honest praise, be pronounced the most triumphant epoch in history. 10 *GEORGE WASHINGTON* For I cannot conceive anything more honorable, than that which flows from the uncorrupted choice of a brave and free people — the purest source and original fountain of all power.

11 *ALEXANDER HAMILTON* The origin of all civil government, justly established, must be a voluntary compact between the rulers and the ruled; and must be liable to such limitations as are necessary for the security of the absolute rights of the people. 12 *DECLARATION OF INDEPENDENCE* To secure these rights, Governments are instituted among Men, deriving their just powers from the consent of the governed. 13 *ALEXANDER HAMILTON* For what original title can any man or set of men have to govern others, except their own consent?

14 *ALEXANDER HAMILTON* It has been observed by some that a democracy would be the most perfect government. Experience has proved that no position in politics is more false than this. The ancient democracies, in which the people themselves deliberated, never possessed one feature of good government. Their very character was tyranny, their figure, deformity. 15 *ALEXANDER HAMILTON* Had every Athenian citizen been a Socrates, every Athenian assembly would still have been a mob. 16 *SCRIBE* For democracy is nothing more than mob rule, where fifty-one percent of the people may take away the rights of the other forty-nine. 17 *SCRIBE* It is two wolves and a lamb voting on what to have for lunch. Liberty is a well-armed lamb contesting the vote.

18 *JOHN ADAMS* Democracy never lasts long. It soon wastes, exhausts, and murders itself. There never was a democracy yet that did not commit suicide. For passions are the same in all men, under all forms of simple government, and when unchecked, produce the same effects of fraud, violence, and cruelty.

19 *JAMES MADISON* Hence it is that such democracies have ever been spectacles of turbulence and contention; have ever been found incompatible with personal security or the rights of property; and have in general been as short in their lives as they have been

violent in their deaths.

20 *ALEXANDER HAMILTON* My friends, in all the numerous assemblies, of whatever characters composed, passion never fails to wrest the scepter from reason. 21 *JOHN ADAMS* For power is a thing of infinite danger and delicacy and has never yet been confided to any man, or any body of men, without turning their heads.

22 *JOHN ADAMS* Any man — the best, the wisest, the brightest you can find — after he should be entrusted with sufficient power, would soon be brought to think, by the strong effervescence of his self-ish passions against the weaker efforts of his social refinements in opposition to them, would soon come to believe that he was more important, more deserving, knowing and necessary than he is; that he deserved more respect, wealth, and power than he has; and that he will punish with great cruelty those who should esteem him no higher and show him no more reverence and give him no more money or power than he deserved.

23 *JOHN ADAMS* All men would be tyrants if they could. The meaning of that maxim, in my opinion, is no more than this plain, simple observation upon human nature which every man, who has ever read a treatise upon morality or conversed with the world or endeavored to estimate the comparative strength of the differ-ent springs of action in his own mind, must acknowledge; that a man's selfish passions are stronger than his reason; that the former will always prevail over the latter in any man left to the natural emotions of his own mind, unrestrained and unchecked by other power extrinsic to himself. 24 *JOHN ADAMS* Thus we must not depend alone upon the love of liberty in the soul of man for its preservation. 25 *JOHN WINTHROP* For unbridled passions will produce the same effect, whether in a king, nobility, or a mob.

71

26 *JAMES MADISON* It has been said that all government is an evil. It would be more proper to say that the necessity of any government is a misfortune. This necessity, however, exists; and the problem to be solved is not what form of government is perfect, but which of the forms is least imperfect. 27 *ALEXANDER HAMILTON* Give all power to the many, they will oppress the few. Give all power to the few, they will oppress the many. Both, therefore, ought to have power that each may defend itself against the other. 28 *MONTESQUIEU* For it is necessary, from the very nature of things, that power should be a check to power.

29 *WILLIAM GRAYSON* Such is the history of the two opinions prevailing in the world — the one, that mankind can only be governed by force; 30 *JAMES MADISON* that, as some say, there is not sufficient virtue among men for self government, and that nothing less than the chains of despotism can restrain them from destroying and devouring one another; 31 *WILLIAM GRAYSON* the other, that humanity is capable of freedom and good government; 32 *JOHN ADAMS* and that government is instituted for the common good: for the protection, safety, prosperity, and happiness of the people.

33 *ALEXANDER HAMILTON* Real liberty is neither found in despotism or the extremes of democracy, but in moderate governments. 34 *ALEXANDER HAMILTON* Thus, we are now forming a republican government. 35 *JAMES MADISON* For as there is a degree of depravity in mankind which requires a certain degree of circumspection and distrust, so there are qualities in human nature which justify a certain portion of esteem and confidence. A republican form of government presupposes the existence of these qualities in a higher degree than any other form.

36 *GEORGE WASHINGTON* A republic is not the phantom of a deluded imagination. On the contrary, laws under no form of government

are better supported, liberty and property better secured, or happiness more effectually dispensed to mankind. [37] *SCRIBE* For in a republic, the constitution is not an instrument for the government to restrain the people: it is an instrument for the people to restrain the government - lest the government come to dominate their lives and their interests.

[38] *JAMES MADISON* In republics, the great danger is that the majority may not sufficiently respect the rights of the minority. [39] *JAMES MADISON* Our government, therefore, ought to secure the permanent interests of the country against innovation, to be so constituted as to protect the minority against the majority; [40] *JAMES MADISON* to be so established as to guarantee the rights of the minority against a majority disposed to take unjust advantage of its power.

[41] *JAMES MADISON* The majority, having such coexistent passion or interest must be rendered, by their number and local situation, unable to concert and carry into effect schemes of oppression. [42] *JAMES MADISON* Ambition must be made to counteract ambition, and the interest of the man must be connected with the Constitutional rights of the place. [43] *JOHN ADAMS* For we are a nation of laws, not of men.

[44] *JAMES MADISON* The powers delegated by the Constitution to the federal government are few and defined; exercised principally on external objects, as war, peace, negotiation and foreign commerce. [45] *TENTH AMENDMENT TO THE CONSTITUTION* The powers not delegated to the United States by the Constitution, nor prohibited by it to the States, are reserved to the States respectively, or to the people.

[46] *JAMES MADISON* Those powers which are to remain in the state governments are numerous and indefinite, extending to all the

objects which in the ordinary course of affairs, concern the lives and liberties and properties of the people, and the internal order, improvement, and prosperity of the state. [47] *ALEXANDER HAMILTON* For there are certain social principles in human nature from which we may draw the most solid conclusions with respect to the conduct of individuals and of communities. We love our families more than our neighbors; we love our neighbors more than our countrymen in general. These human affections, like the solar heat, lose their intensity as they depart from the center and become languid in proportion to the expansion of the circle on which they act. On these principles, the attachment of the individual will be first and forever secured by the state governments.

[48] *JAMES MADISON* Each state, in ratifying the Constitution, is considered as a sovereign body, independent of all others, and only to be bound by its own voluntary act. In this relation, then, the Constitution will forever be a federal, and not a national, Constitution. [49] *THOMAS JEFFERSON* To take a single step beyond the boundaries specially drawn around the powers of Congress is to take possession of a boundless field of power, no longer susceptible of any definition. [50] *ALEXANDER HAMILTON* That state liberties, indeed, can be subverted by the federal head is repugnant to every rule of political calculation.

[51] *JAMES MADISON* In discriminating the several classes of federal power, the next and most difficult task was to provide some practical security for each against the invasion of the others. [52] *GEORGE WASHINGTON* For the spirit of encroachment tends to consolidate the powers of all the departments in one, and thus to create whatever the form of government, a real despotism. [53] *THOMAS JEFFERSON* And an elective despotism was not the government we fought for, but one which should not only be founded

on true free principles, but in which the powers of government should be so divided and balanced among general bodies of magistracy, as that no one body could transcend their legal limits without being effectually checked and restrained by the others.

[54] *JAMES MADISON* My fellow citizens, the accumulation of all powers, legislative, executive, and judiciary, in the same hands, whether of one, a few, or many, and whether hereditary, self-appointed, or elective, may justly be pronounced the very definition of tyranny!

SCRIBE Tempers flared at the Constitutional Convention of 1787 as large and small state delegates debated the structure of the legislative branch. But the tide turned in Independence Hall when Benjamin Franklin stood: [55] *BENJAMIN FRANKLIN* We must consider, gentlemen, that if proportional representation takes place, the small states will contend that their liberties will be in danger. If an equality of votes for each state is to be put in its place, the large states will say their money will be in danger. When a broad table is to be made, and the edges of planks do not fit, the artist takes a little from both, and makes a good joint.

SCRIBE And thus, the Great Compromise created a House of Representatives elected by the popular vote, and a Senate that provides equal representation through the election of two Senators for each state. Likewise, the electoral college was created to respect the interests of all the states in the selection of a President, and as a buffer against majoritarian rule.

SCRIBE As ratification of the Constitution was debated, Anti-Federalists rose up in dissent, believing that the Constitution went too far in empowering the general government, and not far enough in protecting the liberties of the people. The heated debate within each state culminated with the addition of the first ten amendments — the Bill of Rights.

36 GEORGE MASON The question, gentlemen, will be whether a consolidated government can preserve the freedom and secure the great rights of the people. I wish for such amendments, and such only as are necessary to secure the dearest rights of the people. If such amendments be introduced as shall exclude danger, I shall most gladly put my hand to it. *57 GEORGE CLINTON* For all human authority, however organized, must have confined limits or insolence and oppression will prove the offspring of its grandeur.

58 JOHN WINTHROP A Bill of Rights will serve to secure the minority against the usurpation and tyranny of the majority. *59 JAMES MONROE* It will protect liberty of conscience in matters of religious faith; of speech and of the press; of the trial by jury in civil and criminal cases; of the benefit of the writ of habeas corpus; of the right to keep and bear arms. If these rights are well defined and secured against encroachment, it is impossible that government should ever degenerate into tyranny.

SCRIBE George Washington presided over the Constitutional Convention, and as it concluded, recognized Benjamin Franklin for closing remarks: *60 BENJAMIN FRANKLIN* Sir, I agree to this Constitution with all its faults, if they are such; because I think a general government necessary for us, and there is no form of government but what may be a blessing to the people if well administered. I doubt, sir, whether any other convention we can obtain, may be able to make a better Constitution. For when you assemble a number of men to have the advantage of their joint wisdom, you inevitably assemble with those men, all their prejudices, their passions, their errors of opinion, their local interests, and their selfish views. From such an assembly can a perfect production be expected? It therefore astonishes me, sir, to find this system approaching so near to perfection as it does; and I think it will astonish our enemies, who are waiting with confidence to hear that our councils are confounded like those of the builders of Babel; and that our states are on the point of separation, only to meet hereafter for the purpose of cutting one another's throats. Thus, I consent, sir, to this Constitution because I expect no better, and because I am not sure, that it is not the best.

61 *BENJAMIN FRANKLIN* As we have gathered these months, sir, I have often looked at that sun behind you without being able to tell whether it was rising or setting. But now I know that it is a rising sun. 62 *SAMUEL ADAMS* For this day presents the world with the most august spectacle that its annals ever unfolded — millions of freemen, deliberately and voluntarily forming themselves into a society for their common defense and common happiness.

63 *SAMUEL ADAMS* You are now citizens, the guardians of your own liberties. We may justly address you, as the *decemviri*†, as did the Romans, and say: "Nothing that we propose can pass into a law without your consent. Be yourselves, O Americans, the authors of those laws on which your happiness depends." 64 *THOMAS JEFFERSON* For this Constitution will render each of us, and our fellow citizens, the happiest and the securest, on whom the sun has ever shown.

SCRIBE Upon ratification of the Constitution, Article II vested powers in the executive branch, and in the first President of the United States, George Washington. 65 *PRESIDENT WASHINGTON'S FIRST INAUGURAL ADDRESS (PARTIAL)* Among the vicissitudes‡ incident to life no event could have filled me with greater anxieties than that of which the notification was transmitted by your order and received on

---

†   Commissions of ten men established by the Roman Republic.
‡   Changes in circumstances that naturally occur in the affairs of life.

the 14th day of the present month. On the one hand, I was summoned by my country, whose voice I can never hear but with veneration and love, from a retreat which I had chosen with the fondest predilection. On the other hand, the magnitude and difficulty of the trust to which the voice of my country called me, could not but overwhelm with despondence one who, inheriting inferior endowments from nature and unpracticed in the duties of civil administration, ought to be peculiarly conscious of his own deficiencies.

Such being the impressions under which I have, in obedience to the public summons, repaired to the present station, it would be peculiarly improper to omit in this first official act, my fervent supplications to that Almighty Being who rules over the universe, who presides in the councils of nations, and whose providential aids can supply every human defect, that His benediction may consecrate to the liberties and happiness of the people of the United States. No people can be bound to acknowledge and adore the invisible Hand, which conducts the affairs of men more than the people of the United States. Every step by which they have advanced to the character of an independent nation seems to have been distinguished by some token of providential agency; for the voluntary consent of so many distinct communities from which the event has resulted cannot be compared with the means by which most governments have been established without some return of pious gratitude, along with a humble anticipation of the future blessings which the past seem to presage.

As we have pledged on one side that no local prejudices or attachments, no separate views nor party animosities, will misdirect the comprehensive and equal eye which ought to watch over this great assemblage of communities and interests, so, on another, that the foundation of our national policy will be laid in the pure and immutable principles of private morality, and the preeminence of free government be exemplified by all the attributes which can win the affections of its citizens and command the respect of the world.

I dwell on this prospect with every satisfaction which an ardent love for my country can inspire, since there is no truth more thoroughly established, that there exists in the economy and course of nature, an indissoluble union between virtue and happiness, between duty and advantage, between the genuine maxims of an honest and magnanimous policy, and the solid rewards of public prosperity and felicity; since we ought to be no less persuaded that the propitious smiles of Heaven can never be expected on a nation that disregards the eternal rules of order and right, which Heaven itself has ordained; and since the preservation of the sacred fire of liberty, and the destiny of the republican model of government are justly considered as deeply, perhaps as finally staked, on the experiment entrusted to the hands of the American people. [66 *ALEXANDER HAMILTON*] For it seems to have been reserved to the people of this country, by their conduct and example, to decide the important question, whether societies of men are really capable or not of establishing good government from reflection and choice, or whether governments are forever destined to depend for their political constitutions on accident and force. [67 *THOMAS PAINE*] For the cause of liberty is not the concern of a day, a year, or an age; as all posterity are virtually involved in the contest.

[68 *JOHN ADAMS*] It has ever been my hobbyhorse to see rising in America an empire of liberty, and a prospect of two or three hundred millions of freemen, without one noble or one king among them. You say it is impossible. If I should agree with you in this, I would still say, let us try the experiment, and preserve our equality as long as we can.

69 *JOHN DICKINSON* My friends, we must not tamely surrender that freedom which we received from our gallant ancestors, and which our innocent posterity have a right to receive from us. 70 *GEORGE MASON* For it is our duty to transmit to our posterity those sacred rights in which we ourselves were born!

71 *DANIEL WEBSTER* Misfortunes may be borne in our nation, and their effects can be overcome. If disastrous war should sweep away our commerce, another generation may renew it; if it exhausts our treasury, future industry may replenish it; if it desolates and lays waste our fields, they will grow green again, and ripen to future harvests. If the walls of yonder Capitol were to crumble, if its lofty pillars should fall, it can be rebuilt. But who shall reconstruct the fabric of a demolished American government? Who shall rear again the well-proportioned columns of Constitutional liberty? Who shall frame together the skillful architecture which unites national sovereignty with state rights, individual security, and public prosperity? No, if these columns fall, they will not be raised again. Like the Coliseum and the Parthenon, these columns will be destined to a mournful and melancholy immortality. Bitterer tears, however, will flow over these columns, for they will be the remnants of a more glorious edifice than Greece or Rome ever saw, the edifice of Constitutional American liberty.

72 *FREDERICK DOUGLASS* The Founding Fathers, with a sublime faith in the great principles of justice and freedom, laid deep the cornerstone of the national super-structure, which rises in grandeur around you. 73 *FREDERICK DOUGLASS* For the Constitutional framers were peace men, but they preferred revolution to peaceful submission to bondage. They were quiet men, but they did not

shrink from agitating against oppression. They believed in order, but not in the order of tyranny. With them, nothing was "settled" that was not right. With them, justice, liberty, and humanity were "final" — not slavery and oppression. [74] *CALVIN COOLIDGE* If all men are created equal, that is final. If they are endowed with inalienable rights, that is final. If governments derive their just powers from the consent of the governed, that is final. No advance, no progress can be made beyond these propositions.

[75] *FREDERICK DOUGLASS* My fellow citizens, interpreted as it ought to be, the Constitution is a glorious liberty document. Read its preamble; consider its purposes. Is slavery among them? The Constitution contains principles and purposes entirely hostile to the very existence of slavery! [76] *JOHN QUINCY ADAMS* The Founding Fathers, in the Constitution and Declaration of Independence, destined slavery to be banished from the earth!

[77] *THE DECLARATION OF INDEPENDENCE* We hold these truths to be self-evident, that all men are created equal, that they are endowed by their Creator with certain unalienable Rights, that among these are Life, Liberty and the pursuit of Happiness. That to secure these rights, Governments are instituted among Men, deriving their just powers from the consent of the governed. [78] *PREAMBLE TO THE CONSTITUTION* We the People of the United States, in Order to form a more perfect Union, establish Justice, ensure domestic Tranquility, provide for the common defense, promote the general Welfare, and secure the Blessings of Liberty to ourselves and our Posterity, do ordain and establish this Constitution for the United States of America.

[79] *SAMUEL ADAMS* Our unalterable resolution would be to be free! *SCRIBE* For the self-governing American people to be ever alert and vigorously active in forestalling whenever possible, and combating

whenever necessary, any and all threats to individual liberty and to its supporting system of Constitutionally limited government. [80] *SAMUEL ADAMS* It is our duty to defend the freedom of our civil Constitution against all attacks!

[81] *GEORGE WASHINGTON* Let every violation of the Constitution be reprehended! If defective, let it be amended, but not suffered to be trampled on whilst it has an existence!

[82] *ABRAHAM LINCOLN* Let the Constitution be taught in schools, in seminaries, and in colleges; let it be written in primers, spelling books, and in almanacs; let it be preached from the pulpit, proclaimed in legislative halls, and enforced in courts of justice; in short, let it become the political religion of the nation. [83] *ABRAHAM LINCOLN* Let all Americans — let all lovers of liberty everywhere — join in this great and good work. For if we do this, we shall not only have saved the Union; but we shall have so saved it, as to make, and to keep it, forever worthy of the saving. We shall have so saved it, that the succeeding millions of free happy people, the world over, shall rise up, and call us blessed, to the latest generations.

[84] *JAMES MADISON* My friends, the union of these states is a wonder; the Constitution, a miracle; and their example is the hope of liberty throughout the world. [85] *WILLIAM LLOYD GARRISON* Liberty for each. Liberty for all. Liberty forever.

CHAPTER SEVEN

TYRANNY

1 ABRAHAM LINCOLN We all declare for liberty, but in using the same word we do not all mean the same thing. With some the word may mean for each man to do as he pleases with himself, and the product of his labor; while with others, the same word may mean for some men to do as they please with other men, and the product of other men's labor. Here are two, not only different, but incompatible things, called by the same name — liberty. And it follows that each of the things is, by the respective parties, called by two different and incompatible names — liberty and tyranny.

SCRIBE In 1761, the Superior Court of Massachusetts heard arguments as custom officials were attempting to enforce British trade laws against local merchants. The writs would provide legal authority for officials to conduct forcible searches of private property. John Adams was present as James Otis contested the writ, afterwards stating that his speech surely signaled the beginning of the American Revolution.

2 JAMES OTIS I will to my dying day oppose, with all the powers and faculties God has given me, all such instruments of slavery on the one hand and villainy on the other as this writ of government we now endure. It appears to me the worst instrument of arbitrary power, the most destructive of liberty and the fundamental principles of law, that ever was found in a law-book.

One of the most essential branches of liberty is the freedom of one's house. A man's house is his castle; and whilst he is quiet, he is as well guarded as a prince in his castle. This writ, if it should be declared legal, would totally annihilate this privilege. It is a power that places the liberty of every man in the hands of every petty officer. A person with this writ may enter all houses, shops, etc. at will, and command all to assist him. Everyone with this writ may be a tyrant. Every man may thus reign secure in his petty tyranny, and spread terror and desolation around him until the trump of the Archangel shall excite different emotions in his soul!

3 *JAMES MADISON* Since the general civilization of mankind, there are more instances of the abridgment of the freedom of the people by gradual and silent encroachments of those in power than by violent and sudden usurpation. 4 *DAVID HUME* For it is seldom that liberty of any kind is lost all at once. Slavery has so frightful an aspect to men accustomed to freedom, that it must steal upon them by degrees, and must disguise itself in a thousand shapes, in order to be received.

5 *SAMUEL ADAMS* Our greatest danger lies in the subtle and gradual, in the piecemeal approach — by which the foundations are gradually eroded rather than by open and outright assault; accompanied by harsh attacks upon all who seek to alert the people to such danger whenever it threatens. 6 *JAMES FENIMORE COOPER* For it is the habit of public rule to gradually accustom the American mind to an interference with private rights, slowly undermining individuality, and the national character. There becomes so much public right, that private right is overshadowed and lost, the ends of liberty forgotten altogether in the means.

7 *SAMUEL BRYAN* It is to be lamented that the interested and designing have availed themselves so successfully of the present crisis, and under the specious pretense of having discovered a panacea for all the ills of the people, they are establishing a government that will prove more destructive than the wooden horse filled with soldiers!

8 *SAMUEL ADAMS* If the liberties of America are ever completely ruined, of which in my opinion there is now the utmost danger, it will in all probability be the consequence of a mistaken notion

of prudence, which leads men to acquiesce in measures of the most destructive tendency for the sake of present ease. When designs are formed to erase the very foundation of a free government, those few who are to erect their grandeur and fortunes upon the general ruin, will employ every art to sooth the devoted people into a state of indolence, inattention, and security, which is forever the forerunner of slavery. They are alarmed at nothing so much as attempts to awaken the people to jealousy and watchfulness; and it has been an old game played over and over again, to hold up the men who would rouse their fellow citizens and countrymen to a sense of their real danger, as "pretend patriots," "intemperate politicians," rash, hotheaded men, incendiaries, wretched desperadoes, who, as was said of the best of men, would turn the world upside down, or have done it already.

9 *ALEXIS DE TOCQUEVILLE* The foremost or indeed sole condition required in order to succeed in centralizing the supreme power in a democratic community is to love equality, or to get men to believe you love it — 10 *SCRIBE* not simply an equality of rights and opportunity, but an equality of outcome; determined always by power seekers to achieve a result they call 'equitable' through a forced redistribution of property; a leveling of the people. 11 *ALEXIS DE TOCQUEVILLE* For while democracy extends the sphere of individual freedom, socialism restricts it. As democracy attaches all possible value to each man; socialism makes each man a mere agent, a mere number. Democracy and socialism have nothing in common but one word: equality. But notice the difference: while democracy seeks equality in liberty, socialism seeks equality in restraint and servitude. Hence the science of despotism, which was once so complex, has been simplified and reduced, as it were, to a single principle.

[12] *ALEXIS DE TOCQUEVILLE* One finds in the human heart a depraved taste for equality, which impels the weak to want to bring the strong down to their level, and which reduces men to preferring equality in servitude to inequality in freedom. [13] *ALEXIS DE TOCQUEVILLE* The passion for equality penetrates on every side into men's hearts, expands there, and fills them entirely. We can tell them not that by this blind surrender of themselves to an exclusive passion they risk their dearest interests; for they are deaf. If we show them that freedom is escaping from their grasp while they are looking another way, they are blind, or rather they can discern but one object to be desired in the universe. For equality, their passion is ardent, insatiable, incessant, invincible: they call for equal distribution in freedom, and if they can not obtain that, they still call for equal distribution in slavery. They will endure poverty, servitude, barbarism — but they will not endure meritocracy. This is true at all times, and especially true in our own.

[14] *ALEXIS DE TOCQUEVILLE* I am aware that many of my countrymen are not in the least embarrassed by this difficulty. They contend that the more enfeebled and incompetent the citizens become, the more able and active the government ought to be rendered in order that society at large may execute what individuals can no longer accomplish. They believe this answers the whole difficulty, but I think they are mistaken. [15] *ALEXIS DE TOCQUEVILLE* For as the conditions of men become equal among a people, individuals seem of less and society of greater importance; or rather every citizen, being assimilated to all the rest, is lost in the crowd, and nothing stands conspicuous but the great and imposing image of the people at large. This naturally gives the men of democratic periods a lofty opinion of the privileges of society and a very humble notion of the rights of individuals; they are ready to admit that the interests of the former are everything and those

of the latter nothing. They are willing to acknowledge that the power which represents the community has far more information and wisdom than any of the members of that community; and that it is the duty, as well as the right, of that power to guide as well as govern each private citizen. Thus the idea of rights inherent in individuals is rapidly disappearing from the minds of men, as the idea of the omnipotence and the sole authority of society at large rises to fill its place.

16 *ALEXIS DE TOCQUEVILLE* These ideas take root and spread in proportion as social conditions become more equal and men more alike. No man then is compelled to lend his assistance to his fellow men, and none has any right to expect much support from them; everyone is at once powerless. A man's spirit is gradually broken, and his character enervated[†]. For it is in vain to summon a people who have been rendered dependent, gradually losing the faculties of thinking, feeling, and acting for themselves, and thus gradually falling below the level of humanity.

17 *ALEXIS DE TOCQUEVILLE* Democratic nations are at all times fond of equality but there are certain epochs at which the passion they entertain for it swells to the height of fury. This occurs at the moment when the old social system, long menaced, is overthrown after a severe internal struggle, and the barriers of a constitutional republic are at length thrown down, 18 *ALEXIS DE TOCQUEVILLE* as the vices of rulers and the ineptitude of the people speedily brings about their ruin. And the nation, weary of its representatives and of itself, either creates freer institutions, or soon returns to stretch itself at the feet of a single master.

---

† Weakened.

19 DANIEL WEBSTER Good intentions will always be pleaded for every assumption of authority. It is hardly too strong to say that the Constitution was made to guard the people against the dangers of good intentions. There are men in all ages who mean to govern well, but they mean to govern. They promise to be good masters, but they mean to be masters; *20 THOMAS PAINE* men who look upon themselves born to reign, and others to obey.

SCRIBE Men of arrogance: *21 ALEXIS DE TOCQUEVILLE* their admiration for absolute government proportionate to the contempt they feel for those around them.

SCRIBE Men of corruption: *22 JOHN ADAMS* they obtain influence by noise, not sense — by meanness, not greatness — by ignorance, not learning — by contracted hearts, not large souls. *23 JOHN MILTON* They make a heaven of hell, and a hell of heaven. *24 THOMAS PAINE* And when they succeed to government, they are frequently the most ignorant and unfit of any throughout the dominions. *25 ADAM SMITH* Men of systems: *SCRIBE* demanding that society and human nature conform to their utopian visions.

SCRIBE So superior in their hubris; *26 ADAM SMITH* so wise in their own conceit; so enamored with the supposed beauty of their own ideal plan of government, they cannot suffer the smallest deviation from any part of it, and go on to establish it completely and in all its parts. They imagine that they can arrange the different members of a great society with as much ease as the hand arranges the different pieces upon a chessboard. They do not consider that the pieces upon the chessboard have no other principle of motion besides that which the hand impresses upon them; but that, in the great chessboard of human society, every single piece has a principle of motion of its own, altogether different from that which the legislature might choose to impress upon it.

27 DAVID HUME When men are most sure and arrogant, they are commonly most mistaken, *28 ADAM SMITH* ignoring the evidence of their senses to preserve the coherence of the ideas of their imagination.

29 THOMAS JEFFERSON Laws that forbid the carrying of arms are laws of such a nature. They disarm only those who are neither inclined nor determined to commit crimes. Such laws make things worse for the assaulted and better for the assailants. *30 THOMAS PAINE* For while avarice and ambition have a place in the heart of man, the weak will become a prey to the strong.

31 THOMAS PAINE The supposed quietude of a good man allures the ruffian; while on the other hand, arms, like law, discourage and keep the invader and the plunderer in awe, and preserve order as well as property. *32 THOMAS PAINE* For the balance of power is the scale of peace. *33 GEORGE WASHINGTON* And there is nothing so likely to produce peace as to be well prepared to meet an enemy.

34 WILLIAM BLACKSTONE Self-defense is justly called the primary law of nature, so it is not, neither can it be in fact, taken away by the laws of society. *35 SECOND AMENDMENT TO THE CONSTITUTION* A well-regulated Militia, being necessary to the security of a free State, the right of the people to keep and bear Arms, shall not be infringed. *36 JOHN ADAMS* For arms in the hands of individual citizens may be used for the defense of the country or in private self-defense.

37 JAMES MADISON Americans have the right and advantage of being armed — unlike the citizens of other countries whose governments are afraid to trust the people with arms. *38 PATRICK HENRY* Are we at last brought to such humiliating and debasing degradation that we cannot be trusted with arms for our defense? Where is the difference between having arms in our possession and under our direction, and having them under the management of Congress? If our defense be the real object of having those arms, in whose hands can they be trusted with more as in our own hands?

39 *THOMAS JEFFERSON* The spirit of resistance to government is so valuable on certain occasions, that I wish it to be always kept alive. 40 *THOMAS JEFFERSON* For what country can preserve its liberties if its rulers are not warned from time to time that their people preserve the spirit of resistance? Let them take arms! 41 *THOMAS JEFFERSON* For all power is inherent in the people; that they may exercise it by themselves or they may act by representatives, freely and equally chosen; that it is their right and duty to be at all times armed; that they are entitled to freedom of person, freedom of religion, freedom of property, and freedom of the press!

42 *WILLIAM PITT* Necessity is the plea for every infringement of human freedom. It is the argument of tyrants. It is the creed of slaves. 43 *DANIEL WEBSTER* A strong conviction that "something must be done" is the parent of most bad measures. 44 *JAMES MADISON* And these measures are too often decided, not according to the rules of justice and the rights of the minor party, but by the superior force of an interested and overbearing majority.

45 *THOMAS JEFFERSON* Were the government to prescribe to us our medicine and diet, our bodies would be in such a state as our souls are now. 46 *THOMAS PAINE* It is but the greedy hand of government, thrusting itself into every corner and crevice of industry and grasping at the spoil of the multitude. Invention is continually exercised to furnish new pretenses for revenue and taxation. It watches prosperity as its prey and permits none to escape without a tribute.

47 *RICHARD HENRY LEE* The first maxim of a man who loves liberty,

should be never to grant to rulers an atom of power that is not most clearly and indispensably necessary for the safety and well-being of society. [48] *JAMES MADISON* If Congress can employ money indefinitely to the general welfare, and are the sole and supreme judges of the general welfare, they may take the care of religion into their own hands; they may appoint teachers in every state, county, and parish and pay them out of their public treasury; they may take into their own hands the education of children, establishing in like manner schools throughout the Union; they may assume the provision of the poor; they may undertake the regulation of all roads; in short, everything, from the highest object of state legislation down to the most minute object of police, would be thrown under the power of Congress!

[49] *JOHN ADAMS* And when the people give way, these deceivers, betrayers, and destroyers press upon them fast, the encroachment upon the American Constitution grows every day more and more encroaching. Like a cancer, it eats faster and faster every hour. The revenue creates pensioners, and the pensioners urge for more revenue. The people grow less steady, less spirited, less virtuous, the power seekers more numerous and more corrupt, and every day increasing the circles of their dependents and expectants, until virtue, integrity, public spirit, simplicity, and frugality become the objects of ridicule and scorn, and vanity, luxury, foppery[†], selfishness, meanness, and downright corruption swallow up the whole society! [50] *THOMAS JEFFERSON* For when all government, domestic and foreign, in little as in great things, shall be drawn to Washington as the center of all power, it will render powerless the checks provided of one government on another, and will become as venal and oppressive as the

---

† Foolishness.

monarchy from which we separated!

51 JAMES MADISON Citizens! Were the power of Congress to be established in the latitude contended for, it would subvert the very foundations and transmute the very nature of the limited government established by the people of America! *52 JOHN LOCKE* For I have no reason to believe that he, who would take away my liberty, would not when he had me in his power, take away everything else!

53 JOHN ADAMS And yet, human nature itself, from indolence, modesty, humanity, or fear, has always too much reluctance to a manly assertion of its rights. *54 JOHN ADAMS* The most sensible and jealous people are so little attentive to government that there are no instances of resistance until repeated, multiplied oppressions have placed it beyond a doubt that their rulers have formed settled plans to deprive them of their liberties; not to oppress an individual or a few, but to break down the fences of a free Constitution, and deprive the people at large of all share in the government, and all the checks by which it is limited.

55 THOMAS JEFFERSON If it were possible to obtain a single amendment, to depend on that alone for the reduction of our government to the genuine principles of its Constitution, it would be an article, taking from the federal government the power of borrowing. The principle of spending money to be paid by posterity, under the name of benevolence, is but swindling futurity on a large scale.

56 THOMAS JEFFERSON Would it not be wise and just for a nation to declare in their Constitution that neither the legislature, nor the nation itself, can validly contract more debt than they may pay within their own age, or within the term of nineteen years? *57 THOMAS JEFFERSON* Is it not incumbent on every generation to pay its own debts as it goes?

58 *GEORGE WASHINGTON* No consideration is more urgent than the discharge of the public debt. 59 *ALEXANDER HAMILTON* For nothing can more affect national prosperity than a constant and systematic attention to extinguish the present debt, and to avoid as much as possible the incurring of any new debt. 60 *ALEXANDER HAMILTON* For when you allow a government to decline paying its debts — you overthrow all public morality — you unhinge all the principles that preserve the limits of free constitutions — 61 *GEORGE WASHINGTON* and you ungenerously throw upon posterity the burden which we ourselves ought to bear.

62 *BENJAMIN FRANKLIN* Think what you do when you run into debt; you give another power over your liberty. 63 *THOMAS JEFFERSON* To preserve our independence, we must not let our rulers load us with perpetual debt. We must make our election between economy and liberty, or perfusion† and servitude. 64 *SCRIBE* For when the people find that they can vote themselves money, that will herald the end of the republic!

SCRIBE Tyranny comes in many forms. Here is tyranny: 65 *THOMAS PAINE* This new world hath been the asylum for the persecuted lovers of civil and religious liberty. And so it is true, that the same tyranny which drove the first emigrants from their home, pursues their descendants still.

SCRIBE Here is tyranny: 66 *JAMES MADISON* The means of defense against foreign danger has become the instruments of tyranny at home. It is a universal truth that the loss of liberty at home is to be charged against danger, real or pretended, from abroad.

---

† Extravagant spending.

SCRIBE Here is tyranny: [67] *THOMAS JEFFERSON* We must crush in its birth the aristocracy of our monied corporations which bid defiance to the laws of our country!

SCRIBE Here is tyranny: [68] *BOOKER T. WASHINGTON* There is a class of people who make a business of keeping the troubles, the wrongs, and the hardships of the black race before the public. Having learned that they are able to make a living out of their troubles, they have grown into the settled habit of advertising their wrongs-partly because they want sympathy and partly because it pays. Some of these people do not want the black man to lose his grievances, because they do not want to lose their jobs.

SCRIBE Here is tyranny: [69] *GEORGE WASHINGTON* However political parties may now and then answer popular ends, they are likely in the course of time and things, to become potent engines, by which cunning, ambitious, and unprincipled men will be enabled to subvert the power of the people and to usurp for themselves the reins of government, destroying afterwards the very engines which have lifted them to unjust dominion.

[70] *JAMES MADISON* The latent causes of faction are sown in the nature of man. [71] *JAMES MADISON* Thus it is in vain to say that enlightened statesmen will be able to adjust these clashing interests, and render them all subservient to the public good. [72] *JAMES MADISON* For all men are more disposed to vex and oppress each other than to co-operate for the common good.

[73] *JOHN ADAMS* I speak not from the spirit of opposition to government, but the emanations of a heart that burns for its country's welfare. No one of any feeling, born and educated in this once happy country, can consider the numerous distresses, the gross indignities, the barbarous ignorance, the haughty usurpations,

that we have reason to fear are meditating for ourselves, our children, our neighbors, in short for all our countrymen and all their posterity, without the utmost agonies of heart and many tears.

74 *JAMES MADISON* The advice nearest to my heart and deepest in my convictions is that the Union of the states be cherished and perpetuated. Let the open enemy to it be regarded as a Pandora with her box opened; and the disguised one, as the serpent creeping with his deadly wills into paradise. 75 *JOHN ADAMS* For straight is the gate and narrow is the way that leads to liberty, and few nations, if any, have found it. 76 *JOHN STUART MILL* But all bad men need, is that good men should look on and do nothing.

CHAPTER EIGHT

PROPERTY

1 *JAMES MADISON* I own myself the friend to a very free system of commerce, and hold it as a truth, that commercial shackles are generally unjust, oppressive, and impolitic. 2 *ADAM SMITH* For it is not from the benevolence of the butcher, the brewer, or the baker that we expect our dinner, but from their regard to their own interest. 3 *ADAM SMITH* The natural effort of every individual to better his own condition is so powerful, that it alone is not only capable of carrying on the society to wealth and prosperity, but of surmounting a hundred impertinent obstructions with which the folly of human laws too often encumber its operations. 4 *ADAM SMITH* The individual intends only his own gain, but led by an invisible hand, he promotes that of the society. 5 *ADAM SMITH* Thus, individual ambition serves the common good.

6 *ABRAHAM LINCOLN* The prudent, penniless beginner in the world, labors for wages awhile, saves a surplus with which to buy tools or land for himself; then labors on his own account another while, and at length hires another new beginner to help him. This just and generous and prosperous system, which opens the way for all, gives hope to all, and energy and progress and improvement of condition to all. 7 *ROGER WILLIAMS* For when you do what you do best, you are helping not only yourself, but the world.

8 *ALEXANDER HAMILTON* The prosperity of commerce is now perceived and acknowledged by all enlightened people to be the most useful and productive source of national wealth. 9 *GEORGE WASHINGTON* A people who are possessed with a spirit of commerce, who see and who will pursue their advantages, may achieve almost anything. *SCRIBE* But the Constitution only guarantees the American people the right to pursue happiness. You have to catch it yourself. 10 *THOMAS JEFFERSON* And nothing can contribute more to your future happiness than the contracting of habit and industry.

11 *ALEXANDER HAMILTON* All the genius you accrue in life lies in this; when you have a subject in hand, you study it profoundly. Day and night, it is before you. Your mind becomes pervaded with it. Then what people are pleased to call genius, is actually the fruit of your labor and thought.

12 *FREDERICK DOUGLASS* I can explain success by one word and that word is WORK! WORK!! WORK!!! WORK!!!! Not transient and fitful effort, but patient, enduring, honest, unremitting, and tireless work, into which the whole heart is poured. 13 *BOOKER T. WASHINGTON* For nothing ever comes to one, that is worth having, except as a result of hard work.

14 *W.E.B. DUBOIS* And when should you work? Now is the accepted time, not tomorrow, not some more convenient season. It is today that our best work can be done. 15 *HENRY CLAY* For the time will come when winter will ask what you were doing all summer.

16 *RALPH WALDO EMERSON* Labor is God's education. He only is a sincere learner, and he only can become a master, who learns the secrets of labor, and who by real cunning extorts from nature its scepter. I do not wish to overstate this doctrine of labor, or insist that every person should be a farmer. It is merely this: that every person ought to stand in primary relations with the work of the world, ought to labor themselves, and not to suffer the accident of their having a purse in their pocket.

We find our hands full — house, clothes, provisions, books, money — not to use these things, but to look after them and defend them from their natural enemies. They become more than means, but masters. And instead of masterly good humor, a sense of power, and a fertility of resource in ourselves; instead of strong and learned hands, piercing and learned eyes, a supple body, and a mighty and prevailing heart, we become a puny, protected people, guarded by walls and curtains, stoves and down beds, and who, bred to depend on all these, are made anxious by all that endangers those possessions, and are forced to spend so much time in guarding them, that we lose sight of their original use: namely, to help us to our ends, to the prosecution of love; to the helping of friends, to the worship of God, to the enlargement of knowledge, and to the serving of country.

[17] *HENRY DAVID THOREAU* The price of anything is the amount of life you exchange for it. [18] *ADAM SMITH* Thus, the first property which every man has is his own labor. [19] *JOHN LOCKE* That the "labor" of his body and the "work" of his hands, we may say are properly his; that every man has a "property" in his own "person," and this nobody has any right but to himself; [20] *ADAM SMITH* that labor is the original foundation of all other property, and so is the most sacred and inviolable; [21] *JOHN LOCKE* that whatsoever a man removes out of the state of nature, mixing his labor with it, and thus joining to it something that is his own, he thereby makes it his property, annexed to the exclusion of the common right of any other men.

[22] *THOMAS JEFFERSON* A wise and frugal government, which shall restrain men from injuring one another, shall leave them otherwise free to regulate their own pursuits of industry and improvement, and shall not take from the mouth of labor the bread it has earned. [23] *JAMES MADISON* For where an excess of power prevails, property of no sort is duly respected. No man is safe in his opinions, person, faculties, or possessions. This being the end of government, that alone is a just government, which impartially secures to every man, whatever is his own.

[24] *RALPH WALDO EMERSON* When a man who cannot be acquainted with me, taxes me, he ordains that a part of my labor shall go to this

or that whimsical end — not as I, but as he happens to fancy; behold the consequences. [25] *THOMAS JEFFERSON* For soon we will have to labor sixteen hours in the twenty-four, give the earnings of fifteen of these to the government for their debts and expenses; and the sixteenth hour will be insufficient to afford bread. We will live on oatmeal and potatoes. We will have no time to think, no means of calling the mis-managers to account; we will be glad only to obtain subsistence by hiring ourselves out to rivet chains on the necks of our fellow sufferers.

[26] *JOHN DICKINSON* Let these truths be indelibly impressed on our minds — that we cannot be happy without being free — that we cannot be free, without being secure in our property — that we cannot be secure in our property, if, without our consent, others may, as by right, take it away.

[27] *JOHN ADAMS* The moment the idea is admitted into society that property is not as sacred as the laws of God, and that there is not a force of law and public justice to protect it, anarchy and tyranny will commence. [28] *FREDERIC BASTIAT* If the government exceeds its proper limit — if the law gives to one citizen at the expense of another, by doing what the citizen himself cannot do without committing a crime — then we will be lost in vagueness and uncertainty, in a forced utopia striving to seize the law and impose it on all of us!

[29] *JOHN ADAMS* God has laid in the constitution and course of nature the foundations of distinction between men. [30] *DAVID HUME* Thus, if you render possessions ever so equal, men's different degrees of art, care, and industry will immediately break that equality. Or if you check these virtues, you reduce society to the most extreme indigence; and instead of preventing want and beggary in a few, you render it unavoidable to the whole community;

31 *ALEXIS DE TOCQUEVILLE* you render the exercise of the free agency of man less useful and less frequent; you circumscribe the will of a man within a narrower range; and you gradually rob a man of all the uses of himself.

32 *SAMUEL ADAMS* The utopian schemes of leveling and a community of goods, are as visionary and impractical as those which vest all property in the government. These ideas are arbitrary, despotic, and in our government, unconstitutional. 33 *JAMES MADISON* For I cannot undertake to lay my finger on that article of the Constitution which granted a right to Congress of expending, on objects of benevolence, the money of their constituents.

34 *FREDERIC BASTIAT* My friends, when plunder becomes a way of life for a group of people in a society, over the course of time they will create for themselves a legal system that authorizes it, and a moral code that glorifies it. 35 *FREDERIC BASTIAT* For socialists desire to practice legal plunder, not illegal plunder. Like all other monopolists, socialists desire to make the law their own weapon. And when once the law is on the side of socialism, how can it be used against socialism? For when plunder is abetted by the law, it does not fear your courts, your gendarmes[†], and your prisons. Rather, it may call upon them for help!

36 *FRIEDRICH NIETZSCHE* Socialism — or the tyranny of the superficial and the envious — as a matter of fact is the logical conclusion of "modern ideas" and their latent anarchism. Socialists are particularly ridiculous in my eyes, because of their absurd optimism concerning the "good man" who is supposed to be waiting in their cupboard, and who will come into being when the present order of society has been overturned and has made way

---

[†]   Policemen.

for natural instincts. These socialists will not see the act of violence which lies beneath every law they would enact, the severity
and egoism inherent in every kind of authority. They believe it
should be someone's fault that one is suffering — in short, that
the sufferer prescribes the honey of revenge as a cure for his own
suffering. On this logic, revolutions are built. [37] *FREDERIC BASTIAT* Like
the ancient ideas from which it springs, socialism confuses the
distinction between government and society. As a result of this,
every time we object to a thing being done by government, the
socialists conclude that we object to its being done at all. We
disapprove of state education. Then the socialists say that we are
opposed to any education. We object to a state religion. Then
the socialists say that we want no religion at all. We object to a
state-enforced equality. Then they say that we are against equality. And so on, and so on. It is as if the socialists were to accuse us
of not wanting persons to eat because we do not want the state
to raise grain.

[38] *THOMAS JEFFERSON* Citizens! We must prevent the government from
wasting the labors of the people under the pretense of taking
care of them. To take from one, because it is thought his own
has acquired too much, in order to spare to others, who have
not exercised equal industry and skill, is to violate arbitrarily the
first principle of association, the guarantee to everyone the free
exercise of their industry and the fruits acquired by it.

[39] *ABRAHAM LINCOLN* Your property is the fruit of your labor. It is a
positive good in the world. That some should be rich shows that
others may become rich, and hence is an encouragement to
industry and enterprise. Let not those who are houseless pull
down the house of another, but let them labor diligently and
build a house of their own: thus, by example, assuring that their

house, once built, shall also be safe from violence.

40 *JOHN ADAMS* All the perplexities, confusion, and distress in America arise not from defects in the Constitution, but from the downright ignorance of the nature of economy. 41 *BENJAMIN FRANKLIN* For when you offered a premium for the encouragement of idleness, you should not now wonder that it has had its effect in the increase of poverty. 42 *FREDERICK DOUGLASS* You assumed that nature had erred; that the law of liberty is a mistake; that freedom, though a natural want of the human soul, can only be enjoyed at the expense of human welfare, such that men are better off in slavery than they would or could be in freedom; that slavery is the natural order of human relations; and that liberty is an experiment.

You ask what shall be done with them? Our answer is, do nothing with them; mind your business, and let them mind theirs. Your doing with them is their greatest misfortune. They have been undone by your doings, and all they now ask, and really have need of at your hands, is just to let them alone! They suffer by every interference and succeed best by being let alone! 43 *BENJAMIN FRANKLIN* Repeal that law, and you will soon see a change in their manners, industry will increase, their circumstances will mend, and more will be done for their happiness by inuring† them to provide for themselves, than could ever be done by dividing all your estates among them!

44 *THOMAS JEFFERSON* Dependence begets nothing but subservience and corruption; it suffocates the germ of virtue, and it prepares men as fit tools for the designs of the ambitious. 45 *BENJAMIN FRANKLIN* The best way of doing good for the poor, is not making them easy in poverty, but leading them out of it. 46 *HARRIET TUBMAN* We must help

---

†   Encouraging.

them as best we can, so as to lighten the burden on the government as much as possible, while at the same time they learn to respect themselves by earning their own living. [47] *BOOKER T. WASHINGTON* For few things can help an individual more than to place responsibility on him, and to let him know that you trust him.

[48] *THOMAS JEFFERSON* The object is to bring into action that mass of talents which lies buried in poverty; to give every citizen the information they need for the transaction of their own business; to enable every person to calculate for themselves, and to express and preserve their ideas, their contracts, and accounts, in writing. [49] *JOHN HANCOCK* For the more people own little businesses of their own, the safer our country will be, and the better off its cities and towns. The people who have a stake in their country, and their community, are its best citizens.

[50] *WILLIAM BOETCKER* My friends, you cannot strengthen the weak by weakening the strong. You cannot lift the wage-earner by pulling down the wage-payer. You cannot help the poor man by destroying the rich. You cannot further the brotherhood of man by inciting class hatred. You cannot build character and courage by taking away a man's initiative and independence. You cannot help a man permanently by doing for him what he could and should do for himself. [51] *HENRY WARD BEECHER* For it is the heart that makes a man rich. He is rich according to what he is, not according to what he has. [52] *BOOKER T. WASHINGTON* It is character, not circumstances, that makes the man.

CHAPTER NINE
LAW

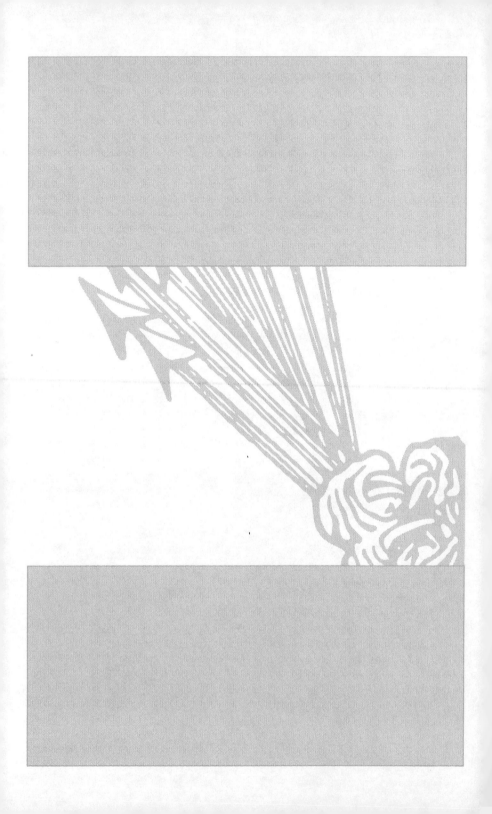

1 ALEXANDER HAMILTON If it be asked, what is the most sacred duty and the greatest source of security in a republic? The answer would be an inviolable respect for the Constitution and laws — the first growing out of the last. A sacred respect for Constitutional law is the vital principle, the sustaining energy of a free government.

2 JOHN LOCKE The end of law is not to abolish or restrain freedom, but to preserve and enlarge freedom. *3 BENJAMIN RUSH* For where there is no law, there is no liberty; and nothing deserves the name of law but that which is certain, and universal in its operations upon all the members of the community.

4 FREDERICK DOUGLASS The Constitution, in its language and in its spirit, welcomes to all the rights which it was intended to guarantee to any class of the American people. *5 ANNA COOPER* For the cause of freedom is not the cause of a race or a sect, a party, or a class — it is the cause of humankind, the very birthright of humanity.

6 THEODORE WELD Society is based on that great bottom law of human right, that nothing but crime can forfeit liberty; *7 ALEXANDER HAMILTON* that every individual of the community at large has an equal right to the protection of government; *8 JOHN JAY* that justice is indiscriminately due to all, without regard to numbers, wealth, or rank; *9 THEODORE WELD* that no condition of birth, no shade of color, no mere misfortune of circumstances, can annul that birthright charter, which God has bequeathed to every being upon whom He has stamped His own image by making him a free moral agent.

10 GEORGE MASON No free government, nor the blessings of liberty, can be preserved to any people, but by a firm adherence to justice, moderation, temperance, frugality, and virtue, by frequent recurrence to fundamental principles and by the recognition by all citizens that they have duties as well as rights, and that such rights cannot be enjoyed save in a society where law is respected and due process observed. 11 *BENJAMIN FRANKLIN* For an equal dispensation of protection, rights, privileges, and advantages is what every part is entitled to and ought to enjoy.

12 *FIFTH AMENDMENT TO THE CONSTITUTION (PARTIAL)* No person shall be deprived of life, liberty, or property, without due process of law. 13 *FREDERICK DOUGLASS* For where justice is denied, where poverty is enforced, where ignorance prevails, and where any one class is made to feel that society is an organized conspiracy to oppress, rob, and degrade them, neither persons, nor property, will be safe.

14 *ALEXANDER HAMILTON* Government is aptly classed under two descriptions — a government of force, and a government of law; the first is the definition of despotism — the last, of liberty. But how can a government of laws exist when Constitutional law is disrespected and disobeyed?

15 *THOMAS JEFFERSON* At the establishment of our Constitution, the judiciary bodies were supposed to be the most helpless and harmless members of the government. Experience, however, soon showed in what way they were to become the most dangerous; that the insufficiency of the means provided for their removal gave them a freehold and irresponsibility in office; that their decisions, seeming to concern individual suitors only, pass silent and unheeded by the public at large; that these decisions, nevertheless, become law by precedent, sapping, little by little, the foundations of the Constitution, and working its change before any one has perceived that an invisible and helpless worm has been busily employed in consuming its substance.

16 *JAMES MONROE* How prone all human institutions have been to

decay. How subject the best-formed and most wisely-organized governments have been to lose their check and totally dissolve. How difficult it is for mankind, in all ages and countries, to preserve their dearest rights and best privileges against the irresistible fate of despotism.

17 *FREDERIC BASTIAT* Here I encounter the most popular fallacy of our times: It is not considered sufficient that the law should guarantee to every citizen the free and inoffensive use of his faculties for physical, intellectual, and moral self-improvement. Instead, it is demanded that the law should directly extend welfare, education, and morality throughout the nation. This is the seductive lure of socialism. Yet these two uses of the law are in direct contradiction to each other.

18 *FREDERIC BASTIAT* Is not liberty the freedom of every person to make full use of his faculties, so long as he does not harm other persons while doing so? Is not liberty the destruction of all despotism — including, of course, legal despotism? Finally, is not liberty the restricting of the law only to its rational sphere of organizing the right of the individual to lawful self-defense, of punishing injustice? 19 *FREDERIC BASTIAT* As long as the law may be diverted from its true purpose — as long as it may violate property instead of protecting it — then everyone will want to participate in making the law, either to protect himself against plunder, or to use it for plunder!

20 *GEORGE WASHINGTON* Should those incited by the lust of power overleap the known barriers of the Constitution and violate the unalienable rights of humanity, it will only serve to show that no compact, no wall of words, no mound of parchment can stand against the sweeping torrent of boundless ambition on one side, aided by the sapping current of corrupted morals on the other. 21 *JOHN ADAMS* Democracy will soon degenerate into such an anarchy

that every man will do what is right in his own eyes, and no man's life or property or reputation or liberty will be secure, and every one of these will soon mold itself into a system of subordination of all the moral virtues and intellectual abilities, all the powers of wealth, beauty, wit, and science, to the wanton pleasures, the capricious will, and the execrable cruelty of one or a very few!

22 *ABRAHAM LINCOLN* And the innocent, those who have ever set their faces against violations of law in every shape, alike with the guilty, fall victim to the ravages of mob law; and thus it goes on, step by step, till all the walls erected for the defense of the persons and property of individuals are trodden down and disregarded. But all this even, is not the full extent of the evil — by such examples, by instances of the perpetrators of such acts going unpunished, the lawless in spirit are encouraged to become lawless in practice; and having been used to no restraint, they thus become absolutely unrestrained — having ever regarded government as their deadliest bane, they make a jubilee of the suspension of its operations; and pray for nothing so much as its total annihilation. While, on the other hand, good men, men who love tranquility, who desire to abide by the laws, and enjoy their benefits; who would gladly spill their blood in the defense of their country, seeing their property destroyed; their families insulted; and their lives endangered; their persons injured; and seeing nothing in prospect that forebodes a change for the better, become tired of, and disgusted with, a government that offers them no protection; and are not much averse to a change in which they imagine they have nothing to lose. Thus, then, by the operation of this mobocratic spirit, which all must admit is now abroad in the land, the strongest bulwark of any government, and particularly of those constituted like ours, may effectually be broken down and destroyed — I mean the attachment of the people.

Whenever this effect shall be produced among us; whenever the vicious portion of population shall be permitted to gather in bands of hundreds and thousands, and burn churches, ravage and rob provision-stores, throw printing presses into rivers, shoot editors, and hang and burn obnoxious persons at pleasure, and with impunity; depend on it, this government cannot last. By such things, the feelings of the best citizens will become more or less alienated from it; and thus, it will be left without friends, or with too few, and those few too weak, to make their friendship effectual. At such a time and under such circumstances, men of sufficient talent and ambition will not be wanting to seize the opportunity, strike the blow, and overturn that fair fabric, which for the last half century, has been the fondest hope of the lovers of freedom throughout the world.

I know the American people are much attached to their government — I know they would suffer much for its sake; I know they would endure evils long and patiently before they would ever think of exchanging it for another. Yet, notwithstanding all this, if the laws be continually despised and disregarded; if their rights to be secure in their persons and property are held by no better tenure than the caprice of a mob, then the alienation of their affections from the government is the natural consequence; and to that, sooner or later, it must come. Here then, is one point at which danger may be expected. [23] *ABRAHAM LINCOLN* The question recurs, "How shall we fortify against it?"

Let every American, every lover of liberty, every well-wisher to his posterity, swear by the blood of the Revolution, never to violate in the least particular, the laws of the country; and never to tolerate their violation by others. As the patriots of '76 did to the support of the Declaration of Independence, so to the support of the Constitution and laws, let every American pledge his life, his property, and his sacred honor. Let every man remember that to violate the law is to trample on the blood of his father, and to tear the character of his own and his children's liberty. Let reverence for the Constitution and laws be breathed by every American mother to the lisping babe that prattles on her lap — let the old and the young, the rich and the poor, the grave and the gay, of all sexes and tongues, and colors and conditions, sacrifice unceasingly upon its altars. [24] *JOSEPH STORY* For the structure of the Constitution has been erected by architects of consummate skill and fidelity; its foundations are solid, its compartments are beautiful, its arrangements are full of wisdom and order, and its defenses are impregnable from without. It has been reared for immortality. It may, nevertheless, perish in an hour by the folly, corruption, or negligence of its only keepers — the people.

[25] *SAMUEL ADAMS* Let each citizen remember at the moment they offer their vote that they are not making a present or a compliment to please an individual — or at least that they ought not so to do, but that they are executing one of the most solemn trusts in human society for which each person is accountable to God and their country. *SCRIBE* And those who do not vote, well, [26] *VISCOUNT BOLINGBROKE* surely indifference must be a crime in us, to be ranked but one degree below treachery; for deserting your country is next to betraying it.

SCRIBE How can the people hold their government accountable if they do not vote? [27] *JAMES MADISON* Or if the laws be so voluminous that they cannot be read; or so incoherent that they cannot be understood; or if they be repealed or revised before they are promulgated; or undergo such incessant changes that no man who knows what the law is today, can guess what it will be tomorrow?

Law is defined to be a rule of action; but how can that be a rule, which is little known, and less fixed? [28] *JAMES MADISON* What prudent merchant will hazard his fortunes in any new branch of commerce when he knows not but that his plans may be rendered unlawful before they can be executed? What farmer or manufacturer will lay himself out for the encouragement given to any particular cultivation or establishment, when he can have no assurance that his preparatory labors and advances will not render him a victim to an inconstant government?

[29] *JAMES MADISON* The effect of public instability, is the unreasonable advantage it gives to the sagacious[†], the enterprising, and the monied few, over the industrious and uninformed mass of the people. Every new regulation concerning commerce or revenue, or in any manner affecting the value of the different species of property, presents a new harvest to those who watch the change, and can trace its consequences; a harvest, reared not by themselves, but by the toils and cares of the great body of their fellow citizens. This is a state of things in which it may be said, with some truth, that laws are made for the few, not for the many.

[30] *JOHN MARSHALL* The Constitution supersedes all other laws and the individual's rights shall be liberally enforced in favor of the individual, the clearly intended and expressly designated beneficiary of the Constitution. [31] *JOHN MARSHALL* Thus a law repugnant to the Constitution is void. An act of Congress repugnant to the Constitution cannot become a law. [32] *JOHN MARSHALL* For the Constitution is either a superior paramount law, unchangeable by ordinary means, or it is on a level with ordinary legislative acts, alterable when the legislature shall please to alter it.

[†]   Clever; shrewd.

33 *ALEXANDER HAMILTON* Those who preach doctrines, or set examples, which undermine or subvert the authority of Constitutional law, lead us from freedom to slavery; they incapacitate us for a government of laws, and consequently prepare the way for one of force. The resistance of Constitutional law is treason against society, against liberty, against everything that ought to be dear to a free, enlightened, and prudent people! To tolerate it, is to abandon our most precious interests!

34 *ABRAHAM LINCOLN* A house divided against itself cannot stand! I believe this government cannot endure permanently half slave and half free. I do not expect the Union to be dissolved — I do not expect the house to fall — but I do expect it will cease to be divided. It will become all one thing or all the other! 35 *GEORGE WASHINGTON* We are either a united people, or we are not! If the former, let us, in all matters of general concern act as a nation, which has national objects to promote, and a national character to support. If we are not, let us no longer act a farce by pretending to it!

36 *WILLIAM LLOYD GARRISON* I am aware that many object to the severity of my language; but is there not cause for severity? With reasonable men, I will reason; with humane men I will plead; but to tyrants I will give no quarter, nor waste arguments. I will be as harsh as truth and as uncompromising as justice. On this subject, I do not wish to think, or to speak, or write, with moderation. No! No! Tell a man whose house is on fire to give a moderate alarm! Tell him to moderately rescue his wife from the hands of the ravisher! Tell the mother to gradually extricate her babe from the fire into which it has fallen! But urge me not to use moderation in a cause like the present. I am in earnest — I will not equivocate — I will not excuse — I will not retreat a single inch — and I will be heard!

37 *JOHN LOCKE* The great question which in all ages has disturbed mankind and brought on them the greatest part of their mischief has been, not whether there be power in the world, nor whence it came, but who should have it. 38 *THOMAS JEFFERSON* And the issue today is the same as it has been throughout all history: whether people will be allowed to govern themselves or will be ruled by a small elite. 39 *THOMAS JEFFERSON* For the greatest calamity which could befall us would be submission to a government of unlimited powers.

40 *GEORGE WASHINGTON* I am mortified beyond expression whenever I view the clouds which have spread over the brightest morn that ever dawned upon any country. In a word, I am lost in amazement when I behold the interested views of desperate characters — jealousy and ignorance capable of affecting a scourge on a major part of our fellow citizens of the Union. It is hardly to be imagined that the great body of the people can be so enveloped in darkness, or short sighted, as not to see the rays of a distant sun through all this mist of intoxication and folly.

41 *THOMAS JEFFERSON* My God! How little do my countrymen know what precious blessings they are in possession of, and which no other people on earth enjoy. 42 *THOMAS JEFFERSON* It astonishes me to find that so many of our countrymen should be contented to live under a system which leaves to their governors the power of taking from them the freedom of commerce, the freedom of religion, the freedom of the press, the laws of *habeas corpus*. This is a degeneracy in the principles of liberty which I would not have expected for at least four centuries.

43 *GEORGE WASHINGTON* It appears to me there is an option still left to the United States of America, that it is in their choice, and depends upon their conduct whether they will be respectable

and prosperous, or contemptible and miserable as a nation. This is the time of their political probation. This is the moment when the eyes of the whole world are turned upon them. This is the moment to establish or ruin their national character forever.

⁴⁴ *SCRIBE* If citizens take liberty for granted; if our culture — molded by journalists and writers, preachers, and teachers — holds other values in higher esteem; ⁴⁵ *SAMUEL ADAMS* if vain and aspiring men possess the highest seats in Government; ⁴⁶ *SAMUEL ADAMS* if men, through fear, fraud, or mistake, renounce or give up their natural rights; ⁴⁷ *SAMUEL ADAMS* if we suffer tamely lawless attacks upon our liberty, ⁴⁸ *SCRIBE* then the spirit that gives life to the Constitution will flicker out!

⁴⁹ *ROGER SHERMAN* And sad will be that day when the American people forget their traditions and their history, and no longer remember that the country they love, the institutions they cherish and the freedom they hope to preserve, were born from the throes of armed resistance to tyranny and nursed in the rugged arms of fearless men.

⁵⁰ *JOHN ADAMS* Citizens! When the people once surrender their right of defending the limitations upon the government, and of resisting every encroachment upon them, they can never regain it! A Constitution of government once changed from freedom, can never be restored! Liberty once lost, is lost forever!

⁵¹ *DANIEL WEBSTER* Hold on, my friends — hold on to the Constitution and to the Republic for which it stands. Miracles do not cluster, and what has happened once, may not happen again. Hold on to the Constitution, because if the American Constitution should fail, there will be anarchy throughout the world!

CHAPTER TEN

CALL

1 ABRAHAM LINCOLN From whence shall we expect the approach of danger? By what means shall we fortify against it? Shall we expect some transatlantic military giant, to step the ocean, and crush us at a blow? Never! All the armies of Europe, Asia, and Africa combined, with all the treasure of the earth in their military chest; with a Bonaparte for a commander, could not by force, take a drink from the Ohio, or make a track on the Blue Ridge, in a trial of a thousand years.

At what point then is the approach of danger to be expected? I answer, if it ever reaches us, it must spring up amongst us. It cannot come from abroad. If destruction be our lot, we must ourselves be its author and finisher. *2 ABRAHAM LINCOLN* As a nation of free men, we will live forever or die by suicide.

3 MONTESQUIEU The corruption of every government begins with the decay of the principles on which it was founded. *4 SAMUEL ADAMS* The warm sunshine of influence would melt down the people's virtue, which the violence of the storm rendered more firm and unyielding. In a state of tranquility, wealth, and luxury, our descendants would forget the arts of war, and the noble activity and zeal which made their ancestors invincible. Every art of corruption would be employed to loosen the bond of union which renders them formidable. When the spirit of liberty which now animates our hearts and gives success to our arms is extinct, our numbers will accelerate our ruin, and render us easier victims to tyranny.

5 THOMAS JEFFERSON Timid men prefer the calm of despotism to the boisterous sea of liberty. *6 ALEXIS DE TOCQUEVILLE* It is difficult to draw a man out of his own circle to interest him in the destiny of the state. *7 PATRICK HENRY* We are apt to shut our eyes against a painful truth — is this the part of a wise people, engaged in a great and arduous struggle for liberty? Are we of the number of those, who having eyes, see not, and having ears, hear not, the things which concern their temporal salvation? For my part, whatever anguish of spirit it may cost, I am willing to know the whole truth; to know the worst, and to provide for it.

8 *PATRICK HENRY* The question before us is one of an awful moment to this country. For my own part, I consider it as nothing less than a question of freedom or slavery. If we wish to be free; if we mean to preserve inviolate the liberty for which we have been so long contending, and which we have pledged ourselves never to abandon until the glorious object of our contest shall be obtained, we must fight!

9 *ALEXANDER HAMILTON* If the federal government should overpass the just bounds of its authority and make a tyrannical use of its powers, the people, whose creature this government is, must appeal to the standard they have formed, and take such measures to redress the injury done to the Constitution!

10 *ABRAHAM LINCOLN* My fellow citizens, we the people are the rightful masters of both Congress and the courts, not to overthrow the Constitution but to overthrow the people who pervert the Constitution. 11 *DECLARATION OF INDEPENDENCE* That whenever any Form of Government becomes destructive of these Ends, it is the Right of the People to alter or to abolish it, and to institute new Government, laying its Foundation on such Principles, and organizing its Powers in such Form, as to them shall seem most likely to effect their Safety and Happiness. For when a long Train of Abuses and Usurpations, pursuing invariably the same Object, evinces a Design to reduce them under absolute Despotism, it is their Right, it is their Duty, to throw off such Government, and to provide new Guards for their future Security.

12 *THOMAS JEFFERSON* Citizens, we are not at once to despair, but to recall the government to its original and legitimate principles and restrain it within the rightful limits of self-government. 13 *MERCY OTIS WARREN* Every American must endeavor to stop the dissemination of principles evidently destructive of the cause for which they have bled, to rescue and save their civil and religious rights from the outstretched arm of tyranny! 14 *JAMES MADISON* Every man who loves peace, every man who loves his country, every man who loves liberty ought to have it ever before his eyes that he may cherish in his heart a due attachment to the Union of America, and be able to set a due value on the means of preserving it.

15 *ABRAHAM LINCOLN* Each of you may have through this free government which we have enjoyed, an open field and a fair chance for your industry, enterprise, and intelligence; that you may all have equal privileges in the race of life, with all its desirable human aspirations. It is for this the struggle should be maintained. 16 *ABRAHAM LINCOLN* For our common country is in great peril, demanding the boldest action to bring it speedy relief. Not merely for today, but for all time to come that we should perpetuate for our children's children this great and free government, which we have enjoyed all our lives. I beg you to remember this, not merely for my sake, but for yours. 17 *DANIEL WEBSTER* For our destruction, should it come at all, will be from the inattention of the people to the concerns of their government; from their carelessness and negligence; from the dupes of designing men to make the people the instruments of their own undoing.

18 *THOMAS PAINE* All who expect to reap the blessings of freedom must, like men, undergo the fatigue of supporting it! 19 *GEORGE MASON* For our all is at stake, and the little conveniences and comforts of life,

when set in competition with our liberty, ought to be rejected, not with reluctance but with pleasure!

20 *THOMAS PAINE* It matters not where you live, or what rank of life you hold, the evil or the blessing will reach us all! The far and the near, the rich and the poor, will suffer or rejoice alike! 21 *SAMUEL ADAMS* And it will bring an everlasting mark of infamy on this generation, if we should suffer our liberties to be wrested from us by violence without a struggle, or to be cheated out of them by the artifices of false and designing men!

22 *JAMES OTIS* The only principles of public conduct that are worthy of a gentleman or a man are to sacrifice estate, ease, health, and applause, and even life, to the sacred calls of his country! 23 *SAMUEL ADAMS* And that time, countrymen, is already come. The calamities are at our door! The rod of oppression is raised over us! We are roused from our slumbers! It is now for us to glut the avarice of the men who have let loose on us the dogs of war to riot in our blood, and hunt us from the face of the earth! 24 *THOMAS PAINE* These are the times that try men's souls!

25 *SAMUEL ADAMS* But if you love wealth better than liberty, the tranquility of servitude more than the animating contest of freedom — go home from us in peace. Go! We ask not your counsels or arms! Crouch down and lick the hands which feed you! May your chains set lightly upon you, and may posterity forget that you were our countrymen. 26 *THOMAS PAINE* For what you have attained too cheaply, you have esteemed too lightly. 27 *JOHN ADAMS* And you will never know how much it cost the present generation to preserve your freedom.

28 *JOHN ADAMS* Posterity! I hope you will make good use of your freedom. If you do not, I shall repent in Heaven, that I ever

took half the pains to preserve it. [29] *BENJAMIN FRANKLIN* For those who would give up liberty to purchase security, deserver neither!

[30] *THOMAS JEFFERSON* But to those who prefer dangerous freedom over peaceful slavery, [31] *THOMAS JEFFERSON* the price of liberty is eternal vigilance.

[32] *THOMAS PAINE* Patriots! Tyranny, like hell, is not easily conquered! Thus I call not upon a few, but upon all: not on this state or that state, but on every state: up and help us! Lay your shoulders to the wheel! Let it be told to the future world that in the depth of winter, when nothing but hope and virtue could survive, that these people, in this state, alarmed at one common danger, came forth to meet and to repulse it!

[33] *PATRICK HENRY* They tell us that we are weak; unable to cope with so formidable an adversary. But when shall we be stronger? Will it be next week, or next year? Will it be when we are totally disarmed? Shall we gather strength by irresolution and inaction? Shall we acquire the means of effectual resistance by lying supinely on our backs and hugging the delusive phantom of hope, until our enemies shall have bound us hand and foot?

[34] *PATRICK HENRY* My fellow citizens, we are not weak if we make a proper use of those means which the God of nature hath placed in our power. Millions of people, armed in the holy cause of liberty, and in such a country as that which we possess, are invincible by any force which our enemy can send against us. For the battle is not to the strong alone; it is to the vigilant, the active, the brave!

Gentlemen may cry, peace, peace — but there is no peace! Our brethren are already in the field! Why stand we here idle? What is it that we wish? What would we have? Is life so dear, or peace so sweet, as to be purchased at the price of chains and slavery? Forbid it, Almighty God! I know not what course others may take; but as for me, give me liberty, or give me death!

35 PATRICK HENRY Were my soul trembling on the wing of eternity — were this hand freezing to death — were my voice choking with the last struggle — I would still, with the last gasp of that voice, implore you to remember this truth: God has given America to be free! *36 JOHN ADAMS* Liberty must, at all hazards, be supported. We have a right to it, derived from our Maker. But if we had not, our fathers have earned and bought it for us at the expense of their ease, their estates, their pleasure, at the expense of their blood!

37 JOHN ADAMS All that I have, and all that I am, and all that I hope in this life, I am now ready here to stake upon it; and leave off as I began, that live or die, survive or perish, I am for the Declaration of Independence and The Constitution of The United States of America! They are my living sentiment, and by the blessing of God they shall be my dying sentiment! *SCRIBE* And on that dying day, *38 NATHAN HALE* I shall only regret that I have but one life to lose for my country.

SCRIBE Patriots! Sons and daughters of liberty! *39 JOHN HANCOCK* We have all one common cause; let it, therefore, be our only contest — who will most contribute to the security of the liberties of America? *40 JOHN HANCOCK* I say again, who will most contribute to the security of the liberties of America? *41 GEORGE WASHINGTON* Where are our people of abilities? Why do you not come forth to save your country? *42 ABRAHAM LINCOLN* For we shall nobly save, or meanly lose, the last best hope of earth!

43 ABRAHAM LINCOLN It is for us, to be dedicated here, to the unfinished work which they who have fought have so nobly advanced; that we dedicate ourselves to the great task remaining before us; that from the honored dead we take increased devotion to that cause for which they gave the last full measure of devotion; that we here highly resolve that the dead shall not have died in vain; that this nation under God, shall have a new birth of freedom; and that government of the people — by the people — for the people — shall not perish from the earth! ⊦⊦ *WILLIAM LLOYD GARRISON* Liberty for each! Liberty for all! Liberty forever!

Dear Reader,

Thank you for reading *The Founders' Speech to a Nation in Crisis*. If you enjoyed the book, please consider sharing your thoughts through an Amazon book review. Reviews are the most important factor in a person's decision to read a book, so thank you in advance for taking a minute to share your thoughts on the bookseller site where you purchased the book.

If you would like to be notified of the upcoming release of the next book in The Founders' Speech series, please visit *www.TheFoundersUSA.com* to sign up for our newsletter. In addition to alerts, you will receive The Founders' Words, a weekly newsletter with quotes from the Founding Fathers relevant to issues of the day.

My mission, and the mission of The Founders USA, is to remind us all of who we are as Americans, of the founding ethos and principles of this great nation, and of the faith and virtues required in a people intent on preserving their liberties. Thank you for joining us in this critical mission.

Steven Rabb

INDEX

ENDNOTES

The notes that follow reflect the sources from which the direct quotations were drawn. As mentioned in the Introduction, some quotations have been lightly edited for the purposes of consistency, correct usage, and flow. While the original meaning and intent of the quotations have been left untouched, for even greater transparency and clarity, the notes will also contain any changes that merit mention. Since virtually every line of this book is a quotation, I have matched the notes to the enumerated attributions within the text. Please note these are also reflected in the index for easy reference.

Finally, I have purposely selected online sources from which to cite the quotation in order to enable readers to quickly locate and read the quotations in their original wording and context. In the same spirit, I have elected to rarely abbreviate any repeated references in order to clearly provide full information for every individual quotation. My hope is that these notes will facilitate and encourage the reader to personally and directly engage with the primary sources of our Founding.

Introduction

[1]   George Washington, Letter to the States, June 8, 1783, Founders Online, National Archives, https://founders.archives. gov/documents/Washington/99-01-02-11404.

[2]   James Madison, Report on Address to the States by Congress, April 25, 1783, Founders Online, National Archives, https:// founders.archives.gov/documents/Madison/01-06-02-0180.

[3]   George Washington, Letter to Benjamin Lincoln, June 29, 1788, Founders Online, National Archives, https:// founders.archives.gov/GEWN-04-06-02-0326.

Chapter One
Liberty

[1]   New American Standard Bible (NASB), The Lockman Foundation, 2020.

[2]   NASB, 2020.

[3]   NASB, 2020.

[4]   NASB, 2020.

[5]   NASB, 2020.

[6]   New King James Version (NKJV), Harper-Collins, 1982.

[7]   NKJV, 1982.

[8]   The Holy Bible, New International Version, Biblica, Inc., 2011.

[9]   Thomas Jefferson, Draft of Instructions to the Virginia Delegates in the Continental Congress, July 1774, Founders Online, National Archives, https://founders.archives.gov/documents/Jefferson/01-01-02-0090.

[10]   Alexander Hamilton, The Farmer Refuted, February 23, 1775, The Founders' Constitution, vol. 1:3:5, University of Chicago Press, http://press-pubs.uchicago.edu/founders/documents/v1ch3s5.html. Original text has "deity" in lieu of "God."

[11]   Thomas Jefferson, Extract from Jefferson's Argument in the Case of Howell vs. Netherland, April 1770, Jefferson Quotes & Family Letters, https://tjrs.monticello.org/letter/45#X3184736.

ENDNOTES

12 Patrick Henry, Virginia Ratifying Convention (quoting the Virginia
    Declaration of Rights), June 12, 1788, The Founders' Constitution,
    vol. 1:14:39, University of Chicago Press, http://press-pubs.
    uchicago.edu/founders/documents/v1ch14s39.html.

13 Samuel Adams, The Report of the Committee of Correspondence
    to the Boston Town Meeting, November 20, 1772, The Rights
    of the Colonists, https://history.hanover.edu/texts/adamss.
    html. Original text has "Colonists" in lieu of "man."

14 Frederic Bastiat, "The Law," (1850), McMaster University, https://
    socialsciences.mcmaster.ca/econ/ugcm/3ll3/bastiat/TheLaw.htm.

15 Thomas Jefferson, "A Summary View of the Rights of British
    America," 1774, Avalon Project of Yale Law School at https://
    avalon.law.yale.edu/18th_century/jeffsumm.asp.

16 "Declaration of Independence," U.S. Congress, July 4, 1776, National
    Archives, https://www.archives.gov/founding-docs/declaration-transcript.

17 Henry Ward Beecher, *Forbes*, https://www.forbes.com/quotes/4239.

18 Frederic Bastiat, "The Law," (1850), McMaster University, https://
    socialsciences.mcmaster.ca/econ/ugcm/3ll3/bastiat/TheLaw.htm

19 Thomas Jefferson, Letter to Isaac H. Tiffany, April 4, 1819,
    Founders Online, National Archives, https://founders.
    archives.gov/documents/Jefferson/03-14-02-0191.

20 Thomas Paine, "Plan of a Declaration of the Natural, Civil, and
    Political Rights of Man," January, 1793, *The Complete Writings of
    Thomas Paine*, vol. 2, ed. Philip S. Foner (New York: Citadel, 1945),
    558. Full text accessible through Internet Archive, https://archive.
    org/details/CompleteWritingsOfThomasPaineVolume2/.

21 James Madison, "The Papers of James Madison," Property, March
    29, 1792, The Founders' Constitution, vol. 1:16:23, University of
    Chicago Press, https://press-pubs.uchicago.edu/founders/documents/
    v1ch16s23.html. Note Madison is quoting William Blackstone (1753).

22 James Fennimore Cooper, *The American Democrat* (Cooperstown, NY:
    H & E Phinney, 1838), 188. Full text available at https://archive.org/
    details/americandemocrat00coop/page/n5/mode/2up. "Liberty"
    used in place of the implied liberty-respecting institutions.

23 Ralph Waldo Emerson, "Fate," *The Conduct of Life*, 1860, IUPUI, https://cspeirce.iupui.edu/menu/library/aboutcsp/emerson/Fate.pdf. The beginning and end of the quotation are from two different sections in this essay based on the implications of fate to liberty.
Essays: Second Series, 1844, VCU, https://archive.vcu.edu/english/engweb/transcendentalism/authors/emerson/essays/manners.html. The middle section is from this essay: "Being a man . . . servile."

24 Robert Ingersoll, "Chicago Speech," Hayes campaign, 1876, https://www.gutenberg.org/files/38809/old/orig38809-h/main.htm.

25 Alexander Hamilton, "The Farmer Refuted &c.," February 23, 1775, Founders Online, National Archives, https://founders.archives.gov/documents/Hamilton/01-01-02-0057.

26 William Pitt, Speech to the House of Commons, London, January 20, 1775, Traditions of the Ancestors, https://www.tota.world/article/1773/. He was speaking in the context of the political philosophy of American Whiggism.

27 Thomas Jefferson, Letter to Henry Lee, May 8, 1825, Founders Online, National Archives, https://founders.archives.gov/documents/Jefferson/98-01-02-5212.

28 John Adams, Letter to Hezekiah Niles, February 13, 1818, Founders Online, National Archives, https://founders.archives.gov/documents/Adams/99-02-02-6854.

29 Abraham Lincoln, Speech at Edwardsville, IL, September 11, 1858, Collected Works of Abraham Lincoln, vol. 3, https://quod.lib.umich.edu/l/lincoln/lincoln3/1:13?rgn=div1;view=fulltext. The first and last sentence of this quotation come from this source.
Fragment on the Constitution and the Union, January 1861, Collected Works of Abraham Lincoln, vol. 4, https://quod.lib.umich.edu/l/lincoln/lincoln4/1:264?rgn=div1;view=fulltext. The middle section comes from this source.

30 "Declaration of Independence," U.S. Congress, July 4, 1776, National Archives, https://www.archives.gov/founding-docs/declaration-transcript.

31 John Quincy Adams, Speech to the U.S. House of Representatives on Foreign Policy, July 4, 1821, Teaching American History, https://teachingamericanhistory.org/document/speech-on-independence-day/.

32 Abraham Lincoln, "Gettysburg Address," November 19, 1863, Our Documents, https://www.ourdocuments.gov/doc.php?flash=false&doc=36&page=transcript.

33 Benjamin Franklin, Letter to Samuel Cooper, May 1, 1777,
    Founders Online, National Archives, https://founders.
    archives.gov/documents/Franklin/01-24-02-0004.

34 John Adams, Letter to Thomas Jefferson, June 28, 1813,
    Founders Online, National Archives, https://founders.
    archives.gov/documents/Jefferson/03-06-02-0208.

35 Abraham Lincoln, Speech at Edwardsville, IL, 11 September 1858,
    Collected Works of Abraham Lincoln, vol. 3, https://quod.lib.
    umich.edu/l/lincoln/lincoln3/1:13?rgn=div1;view=fulltext.

36 Phillis Wheatley, Letter to Rev. Samson Occum, March 11, 1774,
    Pressbooks (thru Virtual Library of Virginia), https://viva.pressbooks.pub/
    amlit1/chapter/letter-to-rev-samson-occom-1774-phillis-wheatley/.

37 W.E.B. Dubois, "Credo," (Memphis, TN: L. Simon & Co., 1904),
    https://credo.library.umass.edu/view/full/mums312-b227-i010.

38 Samuel Adams, The Report of the Committee of Correspondence
    to the Boston Town Meeting, November 20, 1772, The Rights of
    the Colonists, https://history.hanover.edu/texts/adamss.html.

39 Benjamin Franklin, Letter to David Hartley, December 4, 1789, *The Works of
    Benjamin Franklin*, vol. 12, Letters and Misc. Writings 1788-1790, Online Library
    of Liberty, https://oll.libertyfund.org/title/franklin-the-works-of-benjamin-
    franklin-vol-xii-letters-and-misc-writings-1788-1790-supplement-indexes.

40 Patrick Henry, Speech to Virginia Ratifying Convention, June 5,
    1788, Teaching American History, https://teachingamericanhistory.
    org/document/patrick-henry-virginia-ratifying-convention-va/.

41 William Lloyd Garrison, "No Compromise with the Evils of Slavery,"
    speech delivered in 1854, Civil Rights and Conflict in the United
    States: Selected Speeches, USF, https://etc.usf.edu/lit2go/185/
    civil-rights-and-conflict-in-the-united-states-selected-speeches/5061/
    no-compromise-with-the-evil-of-slavery-speech-1854/.

CHAPTER TWO
CONSCIENCE

1   Samuel Adams, "American Independence," Speech delivered August 1,
    1776, Philadelphia, https://www.revolutionary-war-and-beyond.com/
    american-independence-speech-by-samuel-adams-august-1-1776.html

2 George Washington, Letter to members of the New Jerusalem Church of Baltimore, January 27, 1793, Founders Online, National Archives, https://founders.archives.gov/documents/Washington/05-12-02-0027.

3 James Madison, Amendments to Virginia's Declaration of Rights, May 29—June 12, 1776, Founders Online, National Archives, https://founders.archives.gov/documents/Madison/01-01-02-0054-0003.

4 George Washington, Letter to the United Baptist Churches of Virginia, May 1789, Founders Online, National Archives, https://founders.archives.gov/documents/Washington/05-02-02-0309.

5 James Madison, Proposed Amendments to the Constitution, June 8, 1789, National Archives, https://www.archives.gov/files/legislative/resources/education/bill-of-rights/images/handout-2.pdf.

6 Thomas Jefferson, A Bill for Establishing Religious Freedom in Virginia, June 18, 1779, Founders Online, National Archives, https://founders.archives.gov/documents/Jefferson/01-02-02-0132-0004-0082.

7 Thomas Jefferson, "Notes on the State of Virginia," Query XVII: Religion, 1781, Teaching American History, https://teachingamericanhistory.org/document/notes-on-the-state-of-virginia-query-xvii-religion.

8 George Washington, Letter to Col. Benedict Arnold, September 14, 1775, Founders Online, National Archives, https://founders.archives.gov/documents/Washington/03-01-02-0355.

9 John Adams, VI. "A Dissertation on the Canon and the Feudal Law," no. 4, October 21, 1765, *Boston Gazette*, Founders Online, National Archives, https://founders.archives.gov/documents/Adams/06-01-02-0052-0007.

10 John Witherspoon, "The Dominion of Providence Over the Passions of Men," Sermon preached at Princeton, May 17, 1776, Evans Early American Imprint Collection, University of Michigan, https://quod.lib.umich.edu/e/evans/N12065.0001.001/1:3?rgn=div1;view=fulltext.

11 Thomas Jefferson, Letter to Richard Douglas, February 4, 1809, Founders Online, National Archives, https://founders.archives.gov/documents/Jefferson/99-01-02-9714.

12 Thomas Jefferson, Minutes of University of Virginia Board of Visitors, March 29, 1819, Founders Online, National Archives, https://founders.archives.gov/documents/Jefferson/03-14-02-0167.

13 "The Bill of Rights," National Archives, https://www.archives.gov/founding-docs/bill-of-rights-transcript.

14   Edmund Burke, Letter to a Member of the National Assembly, 1791,
     Project Gutenberg, https://www.gutenberg.org/files/15700/15700-
     h/15700-h.htm#MEMBER_OF_ THE_NATIONAL_ASSEMBLY.
     While not verbatim, this quote popularly attributed to Burke
     summarizes the expressed sentiment found within this document.

15   Benjamin Franklin, Letter to Abbés Chalut and Arnoux,
     April 17, 1787, The Papers of Benjamin Franklin, https://
     franklinpapers.org/framedVolumes.jsp?vol=44&page=605.

16   Burke, Letter to National Assembly, 1791.

17   Abraham Lincoln, "Temperance Address," February 22, 1842, Collected
     Works of Abraham Lincoln, vol. 1, https://quod.lib.umich.edu/l/lincoln/
     lincoln1/1:294 ?rgn=div1;view=fulltext. Lincoln referenced "dram-sellers and
     drinkers" in the context, though the observation clearly applies universally.

18   James Madison, "The Federalist No. 55," February 13, 1788,
     Founders Online, National Archives, https://founders.archives.
     gov/documents/Hamilton/01-04-02-0204. Madison is referencing
     unnamed individuals motivated by "political jealousy." Scholars
     are uncertain of No. 55's authorship. It is understood to have been
     written by either James Madison or Alexander Hamilton.

19   John Adams, Letter to the Inhabitants of the Colony of Massachusetts
     Bay, January 23, 1775, Founders Online, National Archives, https://
     founders.archives.gov/documents/Adams/06-02-02-0072-0002.

20   Abraham Lincoln, First Inaugural Address, March 4, 1861,
     The Avalon Project (Yale Law), https://avalon.law.yale.
     edu/19th_century/lincoln1.asp. The prior quotation from Adams
     expands on the content Lincoln's well-known closing line.

21   James Madison, Virginia Ratifying Convention, June 20, 1788, The
     Founders' Constitution, vol. 1:13:36, University of Chicago Press, https://
     press-pubs.uchicago.edu/founders/documents/v1ch13s36.html.

22   George Washington, "Farewell Address," September 19, 1796,
     Founders Online, National Archives, https://founders.archives.
     gov/documents/Washington/05-20-02-0440-0002. Note that this
     quotation along with the three that follow come from the same
     source, but are not in the same order as the original document.

23   George Washington, "Farewell Address," 1796.

24   George Washington, "Farewell Address," 1796.

25   George Washington, "Farewell Address," 1796.

26 Thomas Jefferson, "Notes on the State of Virginia," 1781, Query XVIII: Manners, Teaching American History, https://teachingamericanhistory. org/document/notes-on-the-state-of-virginia-query-xviii-manners/.

27 Abraham Lincoln, "A Proclamation For a Day of Humiliation, Fasting and Prayer," March 30, 1863, Library of Congress, https://www.loc.gov/resource/lprbscsm.scsm0265/.

28 Charles Dickens, *Barnaby Rudge* (London: Chapman & Hall, 1841), ch. 29. Accessed online through The Literature Page, http://www. literaturepage.com/read/dickens-barnaby-rudge-249.html.

29 John Adams, Letter to the Grand Jurors of the County of Hampshire, Massachusetts, October 3, 1798, *The Works of John Adams* (Boston: Little, Brown & Co., 1854). Accessed online at https://classicapologetics.com/a/adlet9.pdf.

30 Edmund Burke, *Reflections on the Revolution in France* (New York: P.F. Collier & Son Co., 1909-1914), paras. 135-136. Accessed online through Bartleby, https://www.bartleby.com/24/3/6.html. While Burke wrote in reference to the National Assembly during the French Revolution specifically, he observed of human nature universally.

31 John Adams (as quoted by Thomas Jefferson), Notes on John Adams and the French Revolution, January 15, 1793, Founders Online, National Archives, https://founders.archives.gov/documents/ Jefferson/01-25-02-0073. Jefferson recorded what John Adams said in a personal conversation after a "meeting of the board for the sinking fund."

32 Edmund Burke, as quoted in *Truths Men Live By* by John A. O'Brien (New York: MacMillan Co., 1947), 191. Full text accessible on Archive. org, https://archive.org/stream/in.ernet.dli.2015.157195/2015.157195. Truths-Men-Live-By-A-Philosophy-Of-Religion-And-Life_djvu.txt.

33 Noah Webster, "Advice to the Young," History of the United States (New Haven: Durrie & Peck, 1832), 338-340.

34 Thomas Jefferson, Letter to Benjamin Rush, April 21, 1803, Founders Online, National Archives, https://founders.archives. gov/documents/Jefferson/01-40-02-0178-0001.

35 John Adams, Letter to Thomas Jefferson, December 25, 1813, Founders Online, National Archives, https://founders. archives.gov/documents/Jefferson/03-07-02-0040. Original wording included "of my little Phylosophy" (sic).

ENDNOTES

36 John Adams, Diary Entry, February 22, 1756, Diary 1, 18 November
    1755—29 August 1756, Adams Family Papers: An Electronic Archive,
    Massachusetts Historical Society, http://www.masshist.org/digitaladams/.

37 Daniel Webster, "Fourth of July Oration," Delivered at Fryeburg,
    Me, July 4, 1802 (Boston: A. Williams & Co./A.F. & C.W. Lewis,
    1882), 12. Accessed online at https://babel.hathitrust.org/
    cgi/pt?id=njp.32101028187985&view=1up&seq=5.

38 Benjamin Franklin, Madison Debates, September 17, 1787, The Avalon Project
    (Yale Law), https://avalon.law.yale.edu/18th_century/debates_917.asp.

39 John Adams, Letter to the Massachusetts Militia, October 11,
    1798, Founders Online, National Archives, https://founders.
    archives.gov/documents/Adams/99-02-02-3102.

40 Samuel Adams, Letter to James Warren, February 12, 1779, *The Writings of
    Samuel Adams*, vol. 4, 1778-1802, ed. Harry Alonzo Cushing (New York: G. P.
    Putnam's Sons, 1908), 124. Accessed online at https://archive.org/details/
    cu31924092891195/page/n149/mode/2up?q=dissolution&view=theater.

41 John Adams, Letter to Zabdiel Adams, June 21, 1776,
    Founders Online, National Archives, https://founders.
    archives.gov/documents/Adams/04-02-02-0011.

42 Samuel Adams, Letter to James Warren, February 12, 1779.
    https://archive.org/details/cu31924092891195/page/n149/
    mode/2up?q=dissolution&view=theater. See note 40 above for more
    information. First sentence comes from this letter.
    Letter to John Scollay, April 30, 1776, The Federalist Papers, https://
    thefederalistpapers.org/founders/sam uel-adams/samuel-adams-to-
    john-scollay-april-30-1776. Second sentence comes from this letter.

43 Patrick Henry, Stamp Act Resolves, May 30 1765, Founders
    Online, National Archives, https://founders.archives.gov/
    documents/Jefferson/03-07-02-0369-0002. Note that the quotation
    was written on the back of these handwritten resolves.

44 George Washington, "Rules of Civility," Rule No. 110, Mount Vernon,
    https://www.mountvernon.org/george-washington/rules-of-civility/11/.

45 The Holy Bible, English Standard Version, Crossway Bibles, 2001.

46 Tecumseh, 1768-1813. While this quote is attributed to him, it
    is disputed and has also been ascribed to other Native American
    chiefs. Find out more information at https://nativeheritageproject.
    com/2013/11/17/tecumseh-die-like-a-hero-going-home/.

47   Thomas Jefferson, Letter to Peter Carr, August 19, 1785,
      Founders Online, National Archives, https://founders.
      archives.gov/documents/Jefferson/01-08-02-0319#.

48   The Holy Bible, New International Version, Biblica, Inc., 2011.

49   Abigail Adams, Letter to Elizabeth Shaw, January 11, 1785,
      Founders Online, National Archives, https://founders.
      archives.gov/documents/Adams/04-06-02-0018.

50   The Holy Bible, New King James Version, Harper-Collins, 1982.

51   NKJV, 1982.

52   Thomas Jefferson, Letter to Thomas Jefferson Smith, February
      21, 1825, Founders Online, National Archives, https://founders.
      archives.gov/documents/Jefferson/98-01-02-4987#.

53   Immanuel Kant, "Fundamental Principles of the Metaphysic of
      Morals," 1785, Trans. by Thomas Kingsmill Abbott, https://
      plato.stanford.edu/entries/kant-moral/#CatHypImp.

54   Benjamin Franklin, *Friends Intelligencer*, 22:47, January 1866. Accessed online
      at https://archive.org/de-tails/sim_friends-intelligencer_1866-01-27_22_47.
      While not verbatim, this quote popularly attributed to Franklin
      summarizes the expressed sentiment found in his writings.

55   George Washington, Circular to the States, June 8, 1783,
      Founders Online, National Archives, https://founders.archives.
      gov/documents/Washington/99-01-02-11404.

56   Popularly attributed to Alexis de Tocqueville's *Democracy in America* by
      multiple U.S. presidents and Sherwood Eddy, *The Kingdom of God and
      the American Dream*, chapter 1, p. 6 (1941). This appears with minor
      variations in *A Third Treasury of the Familiar*, ed. Ralph L. Woods, p. 347
      (1970), as "attributed to de Tocqueville but not found in his works."

Chapter Three
Agency

1   Thomas Paine, *The Rights of Man Part 1*, (1791 ed.), Online Library
      of Liberty, https://oll.libertyfund.org/title/paine-the-rights-of-man-
      part-i-1791-ed. Original in-cludes "irritated" in lieu of "irate."

2   Alexis de Tocqueville, *Democracy in America*, vol. 2, ch 6 (1840),
      American Studies at the University of Virginia, https://
      xroads.virginia.edu/~Hyper/DETOC/ch4_06.htm.

3   Frederic Bastiat, "The Law," (1850), McMaster University, https://socialsciences.mcmaster.ca/econ/ugcm/3ll3/bastiat/TheLaw.htm.

4   de Tocqueville, *Democracy*, vol. 2, ch. 6 (1840)

5   Alexis de Tocqueville, *Democracy in America*, vol. 2, ch 7 (1840), American Studies at the University of Virginia, http://xroads.virginia.edu/~Hyper/DETOC/ch4_07.htm.

6   Thomas Jefferson, Letter to Henry Lee, August 10, 1824, Founders Online, National Archives, https://founders.archives.gov/documents/Jefferson/98-01-02-4451.

7   Daniel Webster, speech to the U.S. Senate, March 7, 1850, Library of Congress, https://memory.loc.gov/cgi-bin/ampage?collId=llcg&fileName=024/llcg024.db&recNum=295. This speech was delivered in the context of slavery and the Compromise of 1850.

8   Webster, March 7, 1850.

9   John Jay, Opinion from Chisolm v. Georgia, February 18, 1793, Founders Online, National Archives, https://founders.archives.gov/documents/Jay/01-05-02-0251. Original includes "unless the African slaves among us may be so called" as a parenthetical aside after "subjects." Such an aside was not an endorsement of slavery, as Jay was a staunch abolitionist, but has been dropped here for context.

10 George Washington, General Orders, July 2, 1776, Founders Online, National Archives, https://founders.archives.gov/documents/Washington/03-05-02-0117.

11 James Wilson, *The Collected Works of James Wilson*, vol. 1, Lectures on Law (1804), Online Library of Liberty, https://oll.libertyfund.org/title/hall-collected-works-of-james-wilson-vol-1.

12 Popularly attributed to John Locke, though the verbatim wording is found in the works of W.E. Channing (see "The Life of Napoleon Bonaparte," *The Christian Examiner*, vol. 5, (Boston: 1828) and "Remarks on the Character and Writings of Fenelon," *The Christian Examiner*, March 1829).

13 Scribe. This quote has been popularly attributed to John Milton.

14 Henry Ward Beecher, *Life Thoughts* (Boston: Phillips, Sampson, & Co., 1859), full text accessible through University of Michigan, https://quod.lib.umich.edu/cgi/t/text/text-idx?c=moa;idno=AJK2188.

15   George Washington, Letter to the Protestant Episcopal Church, August 19, 1789, Founders Online, National Archives, https://founders.archives.gov/ documents/Washington/05-03-02-0289. The first clause is from this work. Letter to the Citizens of Boston, October 27, 1789, Founders Online, National Archives, https://founders.archives.gov/documents/ Washington/05-04-02-0165. The rest of the quotation is from this work.

16   Thomas Jefferson, "Notes on the State of Virginia," Query XIV: Justice, 1781, Teaching American History, https://teachingamericanhistory. org/document/notes-on-the-state-of-virginia-query-xiv-justice.

17   Since this particular quote has been popularly, but incorrectly, ascribed to Abraham Lincoln, I have elected to attribute this variation to Scribe.

18   George Washington, Letter to Mary Ball Washington, February 15, 1787, Founders Online, National Archives, https://founders. archives.gov/documents/Washington/04-05-02-0030.

19   Thomas Jefferson, Letter to Francis Willis, Jr., April 18, 1790, Founders Online, National Archives, https://founders. archives.gov/documents/Jefferson/01-16-02-0203.

20   Abigail Adams, Letter to John Quincy Adams, March 15, 1784, Founders Online, National Archives, https://founders. archives.gov/documents/Adams/04-05-02-0170.

21   Thomas Jefferson, Letter to Alexander Donald, February 7, 1788, Founders Online, National Archives, https://founders. archives.gov/documents/Jefferson/01-12-02-0602.

22   Benjamin Franklin, Old Mistresses Apologue, June 25, 1745, Founders Online, National Archives, https://founders. archives.gov/documents/Franklin/01-03-02-0011.

23   Thomas Jefferson, Letter to Maria Jefferson Eppes, October 26, 1801, Founders Online, National Archives, https://founders. archives.gov/documents/Jefferson/01-35-02-0423.

24   John Winthrop, "A Modell of Christian Charity," 1630. Hanover Historical Texts Collection, Hanover College, https://history. hanover.edu/texts/winthmod.html. Several biblical allusions are referenced. This and the next citation are separately enumerated as they are no longer in the same order as the original document.

25   Winthrop, "Christian Charity," 1630.

26 George Washington, Letter to Bushrod Washington, January 15, 1783, Founders Online, National Archives, https://founders. archives.gov/documents/Washington/99-01-02-10429.

27 Winthrop, "Christian Charity," 1630.

28 New American Standard Bible (NASB), The Lockman Foundation, 2020.

29 Alexis de Tocqueville, *Democracy in America*, vol. 2, ch. 4, trans. by Henry Reeve, Full text through Gutenberg Project, https:// www.gutenberg.org/files/816/816-h/816-h.htm.

30 de Tocqueville, *Democracy*, vol. 2, ch. 5.

31 de Tocqueville's *Democracy*.

32 Scribe. Though the latter half of the quotation is popularly attributed to Thomas Jefferson and reflected in the sentiments found in his writings, this saying originated with Polish writer Witold Grombrowicz.

33 The Bible in Basic English (BBE), Cambridge Press, 1941.

34 Theodore Roosevelt, "Citizenship in a Republic." Speech delivered at the Sorbonne in Paris, France, April 23, 1910, Full text accessible through The American Presidency Project, University of California, https://www. presidency.ucsb.edu/documents/address-the-sorbonne-paris-france-citizenship-republic. This famous speech is popularly entitled "The Man in the Arena."

35 John Quincy Adams, *The Writings of John Quincy Adams*, vol. 7 1820-1823 (New York: The MacMillan Co., 1917), 312. This is the citation for the first half of the quotation.
Adams, "First Annual Message," https://millercenter.org/the-presidency/presidential-speeches/december-6-1825-first-annual-message. This is the citation for the latter half of the quotation.

36 Scribe. Though popularly attributed to James Madison and expressing the sentiment of his writings, we have attributed to quotation to Scribe since it is unverified.

37 James Madison, "Federalist No. 39," January 16, 1788, Founders Online, National Archives, https://founders. archives.gov/documents/Madison/01-10-02-0234.

38 John Adams, "Thoughts on Government," April, 1776, Founders Online, National Archives, https://founders.archives. gov/documents/Adams/06-04-02-0026-0004.

39   Thomas Jefferson, Letter to John Adams, September 4, 1823, Founders
      Online, National Archives, https://founders.archives.gov/documents/
      Jefferson/98-01-02-3737. The first sentence in this quotation (the question)
      comes from this letter; in its context, the revolutionary freedom of self-
      government is alluded to, which is the case here as well.
      Thomas Jefferson, Letter to David Hartley, July 2, 1787, Founders
      Online, National Archives, https://founders.archives.gov/documents/
      Jefferson/01-11-02-0441. The latter sentence originates from this letter.

40   Alexis de Tocqueville, *Democracy in America.*

41   Thomas Jefferson, Letter to Roger C. Weightman, June 24, 1826, Library
      of Congress, https://www.loc.gov/exhibits/declara/rcwltr.html.

C H A P T E R   F O U R
K N O W L E D G E

1   John Adams, Letter to PA., Young Men of Philadelphia, May
      7, 1798, Founders Online, National Archives, https://founders.
      archives.gov/documents/Adams/99-02-02-2450.

2   John Adams, VI. "A Dissertation on the Canon and the Feudal Law," no.
      4, October 21, 1765, *Boston Gazette*, Founders Online, National Archives,
      https://founders.archives.gov/documents/Adams/06-01-02-0052-0007.

3   Thomas Jefferson, *Notes on the State of Virginia*, 1784, The Founders'
      Constitution, vol. 1:18:16, University of Chicago Press, https://
      press-pubs.uchicago.edu/founders/documents/v1ch18s16.html.

4   John Jay, Letter to Benjamin Rush, March 24, 1785, Founders Online, National
      Archives, https://founders.archives.gov/documents/Jay/01-04-02-0031.

5   George Washington, Letter to the U.S. Senate and House of Representatives,
      January 8, 1790, Founders Online, National Archives, https://
      founders.archives.gov/documents/Washington/05-04-02-0361.

6   Jay, Letter to Rush, 1785.

7   Alexander Hamilton, "The Examination Number XIII," January
      12, 1802, Founders Online, National Archives, https://founders.
      archives.gov/documents/Hamilton/01-25-02-0282.

8   George Washington, "Farewell Address," September 19, 1796,
      Founders Online, National Archives, https://founders.archives.
      gov/documents/Washington/05-20-02-0440-0002.

9   Henry Ward Beecher, *Freedom and War* (Boston: Ticknor & Fields, 1863), 112. Full text accessible through the University of Michigan, https://quod. lib.umich.edu/m/moa/ACP3186.0001.001?rgn=main;view=fulltext.

10 Beecher, *Freedom*, 114.

11 Thomas Jefferson, Letter to William Charles Jarvis, September 28, 1820, Founders Online, National Archives, https://founders. archives.gov/documents/Jefferson/03-16-02-0234.

12 Benjamin Rush, *Essays: Literary, Moral, and Philosophical* (Philadelphia: Thomas & Samuel F. Bradford, 1798), Evans Early American Imprint Collection, University of Michigan, https://quod. lib.umich.edu/e/evans/N25938 %20.0001.001/.

13 James Monroe, "First Inaugural Address," March 4, 1817, Avalon Project of Yale Law School at https://avalon.law.yale.edu/19th_century/monroe1.asp.

14 Alexander Hamilton, "The Farmer Refuted, &C." February 23, 1775, Founders Online, National Archives, https://founders.archives. gov/documents/Hamilton/01-01-02-0057. For parlance, the phrase "innate and agreeable" has been substituted for "conformable."

15 James Madison, "Epilogue: Securing the Republic," August 4, 1822, Founders' Constitution, vol. 1:18:35, University of Chicago Press, https:// press-pubs.uchicago.edu/founders/documents/v1ch18s35.html.

16 John Adams, VI. "A Dissertation on the Canon and the Feudal Law," no. 4, October 21, 1765, *Boston Gazette*, Founders Online, National Archives, https://founders.archives.gov/documents/Adams/06-01-02-0052-0007. Adams referred to the British Constitution and ancestors.

17 John Adams, Letter to Abigail Adams, May 12, 1780, Founders Online, National Archives, https://founders. archives.gov/documents/Adams/04-03-02-0258.

18 Benjamin Franklin, Letter to Joseph Priestley, February 8, 1780, Founders Online, National Archives, https://founders. archives.gov/documents/Franklin/01-31-02-0325.

19 Benjamin Franklin, *Autobiography of Benjamin Franklin* (New York: Henry Holt & Co., 1916), Full text through the Gutenberg Project, https://www.gutenberg.org/files/20203/20203-h/20203-h.htm.

20 John Adams, Letter to Abigail Adams, October 29, 1775, Founders Online, National Archives, https://founders. archives.gov/documents/Adams/04-01-02-0209.

21 Noah Webster, "On the Education of Youth in America," *A Collection of Essays and Fugitiv Writings* (Boston: I. Thomas & E. T. Andrews, 1790), Full text accessible through the Gutenberg Project, https://www.gutenberg.org/files/44416/44416-h/44416-h.htm.

22 Samuel Adams, "To the Legislature of Massachusetts," January 17, 1794, *The Writings of Samuel Adams*, vol. 4, 1778-1802, Full text accessible through the Gutenberg Project, https://www.gutenberg.org/cache/epub/2094/pg2094.html.

23 James Madison, "Notes for the *National Gazette* Essays," ca. December 19, 1791—March 3, 1792, Founders Online, National Archives, https://founders.archives.gov/documents/Madison/01-14-02-0144. He references the "class of literati" in the original text.

24 James Fenimore Cooper, *Early Critical Essays of James Fenimore Cooper*, 1820-1822, ed. James F. Beard (Los Angeles: University of California, 1955). The original quote was in the context of fiction as a means of conveying truth from one generation to the next. His focus on the truth found in fiction is grounded in a love for transcendent truth as pursued through the education of the arts.

25 Abigail Adams, Letter to John Adams, March 20, 1780, Founders Online, National Archives, https://founders.archives.gov/documents/Adams/04-03-02-0240.

26 Thomas Jefferson, Letter to Thomas Cooper, February 10, 1814, Founders Online, National Archives, https://founders.archives.gov/documents/Jefferson/03-07-02-0117.

27 Immanuel Kant, "An Answer to the Questions: What is Enlightenment?" September 30, 1784, full text accessible through Manchester University, https://users.manchester.edu/Facstaff/SSNaragon/Online/texts/318/Kant,%20Enlightenment.pdf.

28 Francis Bacon, *The New Atlantis*, 1627, full text accessible through the Gutenberg Project, https://www.gutenberg.org/files/2434/2434-h/2434-h.htm.

29 Ralph Waldo Emerson, "An Oration delivered before the Literary Societies of Dartmouth College," July 24, 1838, *Literary Ethics*, Full text accessible through Virginia Commonwealth University, https://archive.vcu.edu/english/engweb/transcendentalism/authors/emerson/essays/litethics.html. A third "explore" has been popularly added.

30 Frederick Douglass, "Blessings of Liberty and Education," September 3, 1894, Full text accessible through https://teachingamericanhistory.org/document/blessings-of-liberty-and-education/.

31   Thomas Jefferson, Letter to Charles Yancey, January 6, 1816, Founders Online, National Archives, https://founders. archives.gov/documents/Jefferson/03-09-02-0209.

CHAPTER FIVE
SPEECH

1   John Adams, "A Dissertation on the Canon and the Feudal Law," No. 1, August 12, 1765, Founders Online, National Archives, https:// founders.archives.gov/documents/Adams/06-01-02-0052-0004.

2   Thomas Paine, *Common Sense* (Philadelphia: W. & T. Bradford, 1776), Full text accessible through the Gutenberg Project, https:// www.gutenberg.org/files/147/147-h/147-h.htm.

3   Paine, *Common Sense*.

4   Paine, *Common Sense*.

5   James Madison, as quoted by Jay Cost in "James Madison's Lesson on Free Speech," National Review Online, September 4, 2017, https://www.nationalreview.com/2017/09/ james-madison-free-speech-rights-must-be-absolute-nearly/.

6   Benjamin Franklin, "On Freedom of Speech and the Press," *The Pennsylvania Gazette*, September, 1737, included in *The Works of Benjamin Franklin*, vol. 2, ed. Jared Sparks (Boston: Hilliard, Gray, & Co., 1840), 285. The first sentence comes from this work.
Silence Dogood Letter No. 8, July 9, 1722, Founders Online, National Archives, https://founders.archives.gov/documents/Franklin/01-01-02-0015. In his letter, Franklin is quoting from an "Abstract from the London Journal."

7   Henry Ward Beecher, Royal Truths (Boston: Ticknor & Fields, 1866), 131, Full text accessible at https://archive.org/ details/royaltruths00beeciala/page/n9/mode/2up.

8   Benjamin Franklin, "Apology for Printers," June 10, 1731, Founders Online, National Archives, https://founders. archives.gov/documents/Franklin/01-01-02-0061.

9   John Stuart Mill, *On Liberty* (1859), ch. 2, Full text accessible through the Gutenberg Project, https://www.gutenberg. org/files/34901/34901-h/34901-h.htm.

10   Mill, *On Liberty*, ch. 2.

[11] Thomas Jefferson, "Virginia Statute for Religious Freedom," Act passed in 1786, Full text accessible at https://www.monticello.org/site/research-and-collections/virginia-statute-religious-freedom. While Jefferson referenced the "free mind" in this partial quotation, free speech can be inferred from this.

[12] John Locke, *An Essay Concerning Human Understanding* (London: Eliz. Holt, 1690), Full text accessible through the Gutenberg Project at https://www.gutenberg.org/files/10615/10615-h/10615-h.htm.

[13] Mill, *On Liberty.*

[14] Mill, *On Liberty.*

[15] Mill, *On Liberty.*

[16] Mill, *On Liberty.*

[17] Mill, *On Liberty.*

[18] Alexis de Tocqueville, *Democracy in America*, vol. 1, ch. 11, trans. by Henry Reeve, Full text through Gutenberg Project, https://www.gutenberg.org/files/815/815-h/815-h.htm.

[19] Mill, *On Liberty.*

[20] Mill, *On Liberty.*

[21] Mill, *On Liberty.*

[22] George Washington, Letter to the Officers of the Army, March 15, 1783, Founders Online, National Archives, https://founders.archives.gov/documents/Washington/99-01-02-10840.

[23] Benjamin Franklin, Silence Dogood Letter No. 8, July 9, 1722, Founders Online, National Archives, https://founders.archives.gov/documents/Franklin/01-01-02-0015. In his letter, Franklin is actually quoting from an "Abstract from the London Journal."

[24] Robert Ingersoll, "Progress," Lecture delivered in Pekin, IL, 1860, Full text accessible through the Gutenberg Project, https://www.gutenberg.org/files/38804/38804-h/38804-h.htm.

[25] Thomas Paine, *Dissertation on First-Principles of Government* (Paris: the English Press, 1795), 32, Full text available through the University of Michigan, https://quod.lib.umich.edu/e/ecco/004809392.0001.000/1:2?rgn=div1;view=fulltext.

[26] Mill, *On Liberty.*

27   Thomas Jefferson, "First Inaugural Address," March 4, 1801, Avalon Project
of Yale Law School at https://avalon.law.yale.edu/19th_century/jefinau1.asp.

28   John Adams, "Argument for the Defense," December 3—4, 1770,
Founders Online, National Archives, https://founders.archives.gov/
documents/Adams/05-03-02-0001-0004-0016. Adams stated this in
his defense of the British soldiers at the Boston Massacre; he may have
quoted the first part of the quotation ("Facts are stubborn things.")
from Tobias Smollet who translated "Facts are stubborn things" from
a work by French author Alain-René Lesage at a prior date.

29   Thomas Jefferson, Letter to William Roscoe, December 27,
1820, Founders Online, National Archives, https://founders.
archives.gov/documents/Jefferson/03-16-02-0404.

30   Thomas Jefferson, Letter to James Currie, January 28, 1786,
Founders Online, National Archives, https://founders.
archives.gov/documents/Jefferson/01-09-02-0209.

31   James Madison, "The Report of 1800," January 7, 1800,
Founders Online, National Archives, https://founders.
archives.gov/documents/Madison/01-17-02-0202.

32   Thomas Jefferson, Second Inaugural Address, March 4,
1805, Founders Online, National Archives, https://founders.
archives.gov/documents/Jefferson/99-01-02-1302.

33   Thomas Jefferson, Letter to John Norvell, June 11, 1807, Founders
Online, National Archives, https://founders.archives.gov/documents/
Jefferson/99-01-02-5737. "Fiction" was chosen for the original phrase: "…
just as true a history of any other period of the world as of the present."

34   Jefferson, Second Inaugural, 1805.

35   Thomas Jefferson, Letter to Richard Mentor Johnson, March
10, 1808, Founders Online, National Archives, https://
founders.archives.gov/documents/Jefferson/99-01-02-7586.
Jefferson was referring to himself and his administration.

36   Abraham Lincoln, "Full Text: Abraham Lincoln's Cooper Union Address,"
May 2, 2004, *New York Times,* https://www.nytimes.com/2004/05/02/
nyregion/full-text-abraham-lincolns-cooper-union-address.html.

37   Thomas Jefferson, Letter to William G. Munford, June 18, 1799, *The
Papers of Thomas Jefferson,* vol. 31 (Princeton University of Press, 2004),
126-130, full text available through Princeton University, https://
jeffersonpapers.princeton.edu/selected-documents/william-g-munford.

[38] John Adams, "A Dissertation on the Canon and the Feudal Law," No. 3, September 30, 1765, Founders Online, National Archives, https://founders.archives.gov/documents/Adams/06-01-02-0052-0006.

[39] Thomas Jefferson, Letter to Benjamin Rush, September 23, 1800, Founders Online, National Archives, https://founders.archives.gov/documents/Jefferson/01-32-02-0102.

[40] Benjamin Franklin, Silence Dogood Letter, No. 8, July 9, 1722, Founders Online, National Archives, https://founders.archives.gov/documents/Franklin/01-01-02-0015.

[41] Benjamin Franklin, re-printed the Cato Letters from the *London Journal* in 1722, giving a voice in the colonies to the work of John Trenchard and Thomas Gordon, both publishing under the pseudonym Cato. This quotation is from "Cato No. 15," February 4, 1721, https://firstamendmentwatch.org/history-speaks-catos-letters-1720-1723/.

[42] Patrick Henry, "Give Me Liberty or Give Me Death," March 23, 1775, The Avalon Project, Yale University, https://avalon.law.yale.edu/18th_century/patrick.asp. "Liberty" has been substituted for "inestimable privileges."

[43] Thomas Jefferson, Letter to William G. Munford, June 18, 1899, *The Papers of Thomas Jefferson*, Princeton University Press, https://jeffersonpapers.princeton.edu/selected-documents/william-g-munford. Letter to George Mason, February 4, 1791, Founders Online, National Archives, https://founders.archives.gov/documents/Jefferson/01-19-02-0020.

[44] George Washington, Undelivered First Inaugural Address: Fragments, April 30, 1789, Founders Online, National Archives, https://founders.archives.gov/documents/Washington/05-02-02-0130-0002.

[45] James Madison, "The Report of 1800," January 7, 1800, Founders Online, National Archives, https://founders.archives.gov/documents/Madison/01-17-02-0202. In the original context, Madison is referencing the Sedition Act.

[46] Constitution, "The Bill of Rights: A Transcription," America's Founding Documents, National Archives, https://www.archives.gov/founding-docs/bill-of-rights-transcript.

[47] Thomas Jefferson, Letter to John Tyler, June 28, 1804, Founders Online, National Archives, https://founders.archives.gov/documents/Jefferson/01-43-02-0557.

43 Thomas Paine, *Rights of Man*, Pt. 2 (1792), trans. by M. de la
    Fayette, Full text accessible through the Gutenberg Project, https://
    www.gutenberg.org/files/3742/3742-h/3742-h.htm.

CHAPTER SIX
CONSTITUTION

1   Alexander Hamilton, The Farmer Refuted, February 23, 1775, The
    Founders' Constitution, vol. 1:3:5, University of Chicago Press, http://
    press-pubs.uchicago.edu/founders/documents/v1ch3s5.html.

2   Alexander Hamilton, "The Federalist No. 15," December 1,
    1787, Founders Online, National Archives, https://founders.
    archives.gov/documents/Hamilton/01-04-02-0168.

3   Thomas Hobbes, *Leviathan* (London: the Green Dragon, 1651),
    Full text accessible through the Gutenberg Project, https://
    www.gutenberg.org/files/3207/3207-h/3207-h.htm.

4   George Washington, Letter to John Jay, August 15, 1786,
    Founders Online, National Archives, https://founders.
    archives.gov/documents/Washington/04-04-02-0199.

5   James Madison, "The Federalist No. 51," February 6, 1788
    Founders Online, National Archives, https://founders.
    archives.gov/documents/Hamilton/01-04-02-0199.

6   Madison, "Federalist No. 51."

7   Thomas Jefferson, popularly attributed. The Cox Corridors in the
    House wing of the U.S. Capitol building contain an inscription of the
    this quote and ascribe it to Jefferson. The latter half of the sentence is
    included in the Declaration of Independence, written by Jefferson.

8   Daniel Webster, "Second Reply to Hayne," January 26-27,
    1830, U.S. Senate, https://www.senate.gov/artandhistory/
    history/resources/pdf/WebsterReply.pdf.

9   James Madison, For the *National Gazette*, January 18, 1792,
    Founders Online, National Archives, https://founders.
    archives.gov/documents/Madison/01-14-02-0172.

10 George Washington, Letter to Lt. Gen. Thomas Gage, August
    19, 1775, Founders Online, National Archives, https://founders.
    archives.gov/documents/Washington/03-01-02-0227.

[11]   Alexander Hamilton, The Farmer Refuted, February 23, 1775, The
       Founders' Constitution, vol. 1:3:5, University of Chicago Press, http://
       press-pubs.uchicago.edu/founders/documents/v1ch3s5.html.

[12]   "Declaration of Independence," U.S. Congress, July 4, 1776, National
       Archives, https://www.archives.gov/founding-docs/declaration-transcript.

[13]   Alexander Hamilton, The Farmer Refuted.

[14]   Alexander Hamilton, New York Ratifying Convention, "First
       Speech of June 21" (Francis Child's version), June 21, 1788,
       Founders Online, National Archives, https://founders.archives.
       gov/documents/Hamilton/01-05-02-0012-0011.

[15]   Alexander Hamilton, "The Federalist No. 55," February 13,
       1788, Founders Online, National Archives, https://founders.
       archives.gov/documents/Hamilton/01-04-02-0204. Scholars are
       uncertain of No. 55's authorship. It is understood to have been
       written by either James Madison or Alexander Hamilton.

[16]   Scribe. This quote was popularly attributed to Thomas Jefferson.
       Without confident sourcing, we have attributed to Scribe.

[17]   Scribe. This quote was popularly attributed to Benjamin Franklin. Without
       confident sourcing, we have attributed to Scribe. This quotation has been
       cited in *Lost Rights: The Destruction of American Liberty* by James Bovard.

[18]   John Adams, Letter to John Taylor, December 17, 1814,
       Founders Online, National Archives, https://founders.
       archives.gov/documents/Adams/99-02-02-6371.

[19]   James Madison, "The Federalist No. 10," November 22,
       1787, Founders Online, National Archives, https://founders.
       archives.gov/documents/Madison/01-10-02-0178.

[20]   Alexander Hamilton, "The Federalist No. 55," February 13,
       1788, Founders Online, National Archives, https://founders.
       archives.gov/documents/Hamilton/01-04-02-0204. Scholars are
       uncertain of No. 55's authorship. It is understood to have been
       written by either James Madison or Alexander Hamilton.

[21]   John Adams, "VII. An Essay on Man's Lust for Power," August
       29, 1763, Founders Online, National Archives, https://founders.
       archives.gov/documents/Adams/06-01-02-0045-0008.

[22]   Adams, "Man's Lust for Power."

23   Adams, "Man's Lust for Power." Here, "his reason" was substituted for "the social" in the original text.

24   John Adams, Letter to Samuel Adams, Sr., October 18, 1790, Founders Online, National Archives, https://founders. archives.gov/documents/Adams/06-20-02-0254.

25   John Winthrop, Agrippa Letter XVI, Massachusetts Ratifying Convention, February 5, 1788, Full text accessible through https://founding.com/ founders-library/american-political-figures/james-winthrop/.

26   James Madison, Letter to Unknown re: Majority Governments, December 1834, Founders Online, National Archives, https:// founders.archives.gov/documents/Madison/99-02-02-3066.

27   Alexander Hamilton, Madison Debates re: Articles of Confederation, June 18, 1787, Full text accessible through the Avalon Project, Yale University, https://avalon.law.yale.edu/18th_century/debates_618.asp.

28   Montesquieu, *The Spirit of the Laws* (1748), trans. by Thomas Nugent, The Founders' Constitution, vol. 1:17:9, University of Chicago Press, https:// press-pubs.uchicago.edu/founders/documents/v1ch17s9.html.

29   William Grayson, Speech on June 11, 1788, *The Debates in the Several State Conventions on the Adoption of the Federal Constitution* (Philadelphia, 1876), vol. 3, Full text accessible through the Online Library of Liberty, https://oll. libertyfund.org/title/elliot-the-debates-in-the-several-state-conventions-vol-3.

30   James Madison, "The Federalist No. 55," February 13, 1788, Founders Online, National Archives, https://founders.archives. gov/documents/Hamilton/01-04-02-0204. Scholars are uncertain of No. 55's authorship. It is understood to have been written by either James Madison or Alexander Hamilton.

31   Grayson, Speech on June 11, 1788.

32   John Adams, The Report of a Constitution or Form of Government for the Commonwealth of Massachusetts, October 28-31, 1779, Founders Online, National Archives, https://founders. archives.gov/documents/Adams/06-08-02-0161-0002.

33   Alexander Hamilton, Constitutional Convention, Remarks on the Term of Office for Members of the Second Branch of the Legislature, June 26, 1787, Founders Online, National Archives, https:// founders.archives.gov/documents/Hamilton/01-04-02-0108.

34   Hamilton, Constitutional Convention, 1787.

35   Madison, "Federalist No. 55."

36   George Washington, Letter to Edmund Pendleton, January 22, 1795,
     Founders Online, National Archives, https://founders.archives.gov/
     documents/Washington/05-17-02-0282. "Constitutional republic"
     has been substituted here for the original "republicanism."

37   Scribe. This quote was popularly attributed to Patrick Henry.
     Without confident sourcing, we have attributed it to Scribe.

38   James Madison, "Speech in the Virginia Convention," December 2, 1829, Full
     text accessible through *Rotunda*, University of Virginia Press, https://rotunda.
     upress.virginia.edu/founders/default.xqy?keys=FOEA-print-02-02-02-1924.

39   James Madison, "Term of the Senate," June 26, 1787,
     Founders Online, National Archives, https://founders.
     archives.gov/documents/Madison/01-10-02-0044.

40   Madison, "Virginia Convention," 1829.

41   Madison, "The Federalist No. 10," November 22, 1787
     Founders Online, National Archives, https://founders.
     archives.gov/documents/Madison/01-10-02-0178.

42   James Madison, "The Federalist No. 51," February 6, 1788,
     Founders Online, National Archives, https://founders.
     archives.gov/documents/Hamilton/01-04-02-0199.

43   John Adams, as Novenglus, Open Letter to the Inhabitants of the
     Colony of Massachusetts Bay, March 6, 1775, Full text accessible
     through the Gutenberg Project, https://www.gutenberg.org/
     files/45205/45205-h/45205-h.htm. Adams' original statement included
     "government" for "nation," though he was referencing a quote from
     James Harrington who used the term "empire" in the same place.

44   James Madison, "The Federalist No. 45," January 26, 1788,
     Founders Online, National Archives, https://founders.
     archives.gov/documents/Madison/01-10-02-0254.

45   The Constitution of the United States, National Archives, https://
     www.archives.gov/founding-docs/constitution-transcript.

46   Madison, "Federalist No. 45," 1788.

47   Alexander Hamilton, Remarks at the New York Ratifying Convention
     (Francis Childs' version), June 27, 1788, Founders Online, National Archives,
     https://founders.archives.gov/documents/Hamilton/01-05-02-0012-0034.

48   James Madison, "Federalist No. 39," January 16, 1788,
      Founders Online, National Archives, https://founders.
      archives.gov/documents/Madison/01-10-02-0234.

49   Thomas Jefferson, Opinion on the Constitutionality of the Bill for Establishing
      a National Bank, February 15, 1791, Founders Online, National Archives,
      https://founders.archives.gov/documents/Jefferson/01-19-02-0051.

50   Alexander Hamilton, New York Convention, 1788.

51   James Madison, "Federalist No. 48," February 1, 1788,
      Founders Online, National Archives, https://founders.
      archives.gov/documents/Madison/01-10-02-0269.

52   George Washington, "Farewell Address," September 19, 1796,
      Founders Online National Archives, https://founders.archives.
      gov/documents/Washington/05-20-02-0440-0002.

53   Thomas Jefferson, *Notes on the State of Virginia*, 1784, Query XVIII, The
      Founders' Constitution, col. 1:10:9, University of Chicago Press, https://
      press-pubs.uchicago.edu/founders/documents/v1ch10s9.html.

54   James Madison, "Federalist No. 47," January 30, 1788,
      Founders Online, National Archives, https://founders.
      archives.gov/documents/Madison/01-10-02-0266.

55   Benjamin Franklin, Madison Debates, June 30, 1787, The Avalon Project
      (Yale Law), https://avalon.law.yale.edu/18th_century/debates_630.asp.

56   George Mason, Virginia Ratifying Convention, June 4, 1788, Full text accessible
      through the Center for the Study of the American Constitution, University of
      Wisconsin, https://archive.csac.history.wisc.edu/George_Mason_Speech(1).pdf.

57   George Clinton, "Antifederalist No. 3," March 7, 1788, originally
      printed in the *Maryland Gazette* and *Baltimore Advertiser*, Full text accessible
      through the University of Tulsa, http://resources.utulsa.edu/law/
      classes/rice/Constitutional/AntiFederalist/03.htm. The exact author
      of this anonymously published letter ("A Farmer") is unknown; Clinton's
      contemporaries (Robert Yates and Samuel Bryan) also penned letters,
      but the general consensus is that Clinton authored this letter.

58   John Winthrop, Agrippa Letter XVI, Massachusetts Ratifying Convention,
      February 5, 1788, Full text accessible through https://founding.com/
      founders-library/american-political-figures/james-winthrop/.

59   James Monroe, "Notes on a Constitution for France," Paris, 1795,
      James Monroe Papers, Manuscripts, & Archives Division, The New York
      Public Library (Astor, Lennox, and Tilden Foundations).

[60] Benjamin Franklin, Madison Debates, September 17, 1787, Full text accessible through the Avalon Project, Yale University, https://avalon.law.yale.edu/18th_century/debates_917.asp.

[61] Franklin, Debates, 1787.

[62] Samuel Adams, "On American Independence," August 1, 1776, Philadelphia, Text accessible through Bartleby, https://www.bartleby.com/268/8/18.html.

[63] Adams, "Independence," 1776.

[64] Thomas Jefferson, Letter to John Adams, October 28, 1813, Founders Online, National Archives, https://founders.archives.gov/documents/Jefferson/03-06-02-0446.

[65] George Washington, "First Inaugural Address," April 30, 1789, National Archives, https://www.archives.gov/exhibits/american_originals/inaugtxt.html.

[66] Alexander Hamilton, "The Federalist No. 1," October 27, 1787, Founders Online, National Archives, https://founders.archives.gov/documents/Hamilton/01-04-02-0152.

[67] Thomas Paine, *Common Sense* (Philadelphia: W. & T. Bradford, 1776), Full text accessible through the Gutenberg Project, https://www.gutenberg.org/files/147/147-h/147-h.htm.

[68] John Adams, Letter to the Comte de Sarsfield, February 3, 1786, Founders Online, National Archives, https://founders.archives.gov/documents/Adams/06-18-02-0069.

[69] John Dickinson, "Declaration on Taking Arms," July 6, 1775, Continental Congress, Full text of both Thomas Jefferson's and John Dickinson's drafts are accessible through the Avalon Project, Yale University, https://avalon.law.yale.edu/18th_century/contcong_07-06-75.asp.

[70] George Mason, "Last Will & Testament," March 20, 1773, Full text accessible through the Constitutional Sources Project, https://www.consource.org/document/george-masons-last-will-and-testament-1773-3-20/.

[71] Daniel Webster, "The Character of Washington," February 22, 1832, Full text accessible American Literature.com, https://americanliterature.com/history/daniel-webster/speech/the-character-of-washington.

[72] Frederick Douglass, "What to the Slave is the Fourth of July," July 5, 1852, Rochester Ladies' Anti-Slavery Society, Full text accessible through the National Endowment for the Humanities, https://edsitement.neh.gov/student-activities/frederick-douglasss-what-slave-fourth-july.

73 Douglass, "What to the Slave," 1852.

74 Calvin Coolidge, "The Inspiration of the Declaration of Independence," July 5, 1926, Philadelphia, Full text accessed through the Coolidge Foundation, https://coolidgefoundation.org/resources/inspiration-of-the-declaration-of-independence/.

75 Douglass, "What to the Slave," 1852.

76 John Quincy Adams, *An Oration Delivered Before the Inhabitants of the Town of Newburyport* (Newburyport: Morss & Brewster, 1837), 50. Full text accessible at Archive.org, https://archive.org/details/orationdelivered00adam/page/50/mode/2up.

77 "Declaration of Independence," U.S. Congress, July 4, 1776, National Archives, https://www.archives.gov/founding-docs/declaration-transcript.

78 The Constitution of the United States, National Archives, https://www.archives.gov/founding-docs/constitution-transcript.

79 Samuel Adams, Letter to James Warren, April 16, 1776, *Warren-Adams Letters*, vol. 1 (1743-1777), Massachusetts Historical Society, vol. 72, https://babel.hathitrust.org/cgi/pt?id=dul1.ark:/13960/t3kw93x2k&view=1up&seq=279.

80 Samuel Adams, The Report of the Committee of Correspondence to the Boston Town Meeting, November 20, 1772, "The Rights of the Colonists," https://history.hanover.edu/texts/adamss.html.

81 George Washington, Letter to Henry Lee, Jr., October 31, 1786, Founders Online, National Archives, https://founders.archives.gov/documents/Washington/04-04-02-0286.

82 Abraham Lincoln, "The Perpetuation of Our Political Institutions," January 27, 1838, delivered to the Young Men's Lyceum of Springfield, Full text accessible through the University of Michigan, https://quod.lib.umich.edu/j/jala/2629860.0006.103/--perpetuation-of-our-political-institutions-address.

83 Abraham Lincoln, Peoria Speech, October 16, 1854, Full text accessible through the National Park Service, https://www.nps.gov/liho/learn/historyculture/peoriaspeech.htm.

84 James Madison, *The Writings of James Madison*, The Founders' Constitution, vol. 1:7:27, University of Chicago Press, https://press-pubs.uchicago.edu/founders/documents/v1ch7s27.html.

[85] William Lloyd Garrison, "No Compromise with the Evils of Slavery,"
speech delivered in 1854, Civil Rights and Conflict in the United
States: Selected Speeches, USF, https://etc.usf.edu/lit2go/185/
civil-rights-and-conflict-in-the-united-states-selected-speeches/5061/
no-compromise-with-the-evil-of-slavery-speech-1854/.

CHAPTER SEVEN
TYRANNY

[1] Abraham Lincoln, Address at Sanitary Fair in Baltimore, Maryland, April
18, 1864, Full text accessible through the University of Michigan, https://
quod.lib.umich.edu/l/lincoln/lincoln7/1:665?rgn=div1;singlegenre=All;sort
=occur;subview=detail;type=simple;view=fulltext;q1=april+18+1864.

[2] James Otis, "Against Writs of Assistance," February 24, 1761, Full
text accessible through the University of Pennsylvania, https://www.
sas.upenn.edu/~cavitch/pdf-library/Otis_Against%20Writs.pdf.

[3] James Madison, "General Defense of the Constitution," June
6, 1788, Founders Online, National Archives, https://founders.
archives.gov/documents/Madison/01-11-02-0062.

[4] David Hume, "Of the Liberty of the Press," *Essays Moral, Political, and Literary*
(1742), The Founders' Constitution, vol. 5:1:2, University of Chicago Press,
https://press-pubs.uchicago.edu/founders/documents/amendI_speechs2.html.

[5] Samuel Adams, Letter to the *Boston Gazette* as "Candidus,"
April 10, 1773, Samuel Adams Heritage Society, http://www.
samuel-adams-heritage.com/documents/candidus.html.

[6] James Fenimore Cooper, *The American Democrat* (Cooperstown, NY:
H & E Phinney, 1838), 183. Full text available at https://archive.
org/details/americandemocrat00coop/page/n5/mode/2up.

[7] Samuel Bryan, Anti-Federalist Papers, Centinel IV, published in
The Independent Gazette, November 30, 1787, Full text accessible
through the University of Michigan, https://quod.lib.umich.
edu/e/evans/N16599.0001.001/1:7?rgn=div1;view=fulltext.

[8] Samuel Adams, Letter to the *Boston Gazette*, December 9, 1771, *The Writings of
Samuel Adams*, vol. 2 1770-1773, ed. Harry Alonzo Cushing (G.P. Putnam's Sons:
New York, 1906), 255. Full text accessible through https://ia800203.us.archive.
org/5/items/writitngssamadam02adamrich/writitngssamadam02adamrich.pdf.

ENDNOTES

9   Alexis de Tocqueville, *Democracy in America*, vol. 2, trans. by
Henry Reeve, Full text through Gutenberg Project, https://
www.gutenberg.org/files/816/816-h/816-h.htm.

10   Scribe, though popularly attributed to Benjamin Franklin.

11   de Tocqueville, Constituent Assembly speech, September 12, 1848, trans. by
Ronald Hamowy, full text accessible through the Online Library of Liberty,
https://oll.libertyfund.org/page/tocqueville-s-critique-of-socialism-1848.

12   de Tocqueville, *Democracy*, vol. 1, trans. by Henry Reeve, Full text through
Gutenberg Project, https://www.gutenberg.org/files/815/815-h/815-h.htm.

13   de Tocqueville, *Democracy*, vol. 2.

14   de Tocqueville, *Democracy*, vol. 2.

15   de Tocqueville, *Democracy*, vol. 2.

16   de Tocqueville, *Democracy*, vol. 2.

17   de Tocqueville, *Democracy*, vol. 2. "Constitutional republic" has
been substituted for "rank" that was used in the original text.

18   de Tocqueville, *Democracy*, vol. 2.

19   Daniel Webster, Speech delivered at Niblo's Saloon in New York, March
15, 1837, Full text accessible through the University of Pittsburgh, https://
digital.library.pitt.edu/islandora/object/pitt%3A31735054847664/.

20   Thomas Paine, *Common Sense* (Philadelphia: W. & T. Bradford,
1776), Full text accessible through the Gutenberg Project, https://
www.gutenberg.org/files/147/147-h/147-h.htm.

21   Alexis de Tocqueville, *The Old Regime and the Revolution* (New York: Harper and
Brothers, 1856), xi, Full text accessible through Archive.org, https://archive.
org/details/cu31924014201044/page/n5/mode/2up?ref=ol&view=theater.

22   John Adams, Letter to James Warren, April 22, 1776,
Founders Online, National Archives, https://founders.
archives.gov/documents/Adams/06-04-02-0052.

23   John Milton, *Paradise Lost* (London, 1667), Book 1, Full text accessible
through the Gutenberg Project, https://www.gutenberg.org/files/26/26-
h/26-h.htm. The original lines read: "The mind is its own place,
and in itself/Can make a Heaven of Hell, a Hell of Heaven."

24   Thomas Paine, *Common Sense* (Philadelphia: W. & T. Bradford,
     1776), Full text accessible through the Gutenberg Project, https://
     www.gutenberg.org/files/147/147-h/147-h.htm.

25   Adam Smith, "The Theory of Moral Sentiments," *The Essays of Adam Smith*
     (London: Alex Murray & Co., 1872), Full text accessible through the University
     of Michigan, https://www.gutenberg.org/files/58559/58559-h/58559-h.htm.

26   Smith, "Moral Sentiments."

27   David Hume, *An Enquiry Concerning the Principles of Morals* (London,
     1751), Full text accessible through the Gutenberg Project, https://
     www.gutenberg.org/files/4320/4320-h/4320-h.htm.

28   Adam Smith, "The Principles which Lead and Direct Philosophical
     Enquiries," *The Essays of Adam Smith* (London: Alex Murray & Co., 1872),
     Full text accessible through the University of Michigan, https://www.
     gutenberg.org/files/58559/58559-h/58559-h.htm. Quote marks added.

29   Thomas Jefferson, *Jefferson's Legal Commonplace Book* (1762-1767), eds.
     David Konig and Michael Zuckert (Princeton: Princeton University
     Press, 2019), 521. Jefferson had documented this quotation from Ceasare
     Beccaria in the original Italian. When publishing copies of his private legal
     reference book for the public, editors translated the quote into English.

30   Thomas Paine, "Thoughts on Defensive War," *Pennsylvania Magazine* (July,
     1775), Full text accessible through the Online Library of Liberty, https://oll.
     libertyfund.org/title/paine-the-writings-of-thomas-paine-vol-i-1774-1779.

31   Paine, "Defensive War."

32   Paine, "Defensive War."

33   George Washington, Letter to Elbridge Gerry, January 29,
     1780, Founders Online, National Archives, https://founders.
     archives.gov/documents/Washington/03-24-02-0242.

34   William Blackstone, *Commentaries on Laws of England*, Book 3
     (Worcester, MA: Isaiah Thomas, 1790), Full text accessible thought
     the Online Library of Liberty, https://oll.libertyfund.org/title/
     sharswood-commentaries-on-the-laws-of-england-in-four-books-vol-2.

35   The Constitution of the United States, National Archives, https://
     www.archives.gov/founding-docs/constitution-transcript.

36 John Adams, "A Defence of the Constitutions of Government," vol. I-III, Text accessible through the Online Library of Liberty, https://oll.libertyfund.org/title/adams-the-works-of-john-adams-vol-5-defence-of-the-constitutions-vols-ii-and-iii.

37 James Madison, "The Federalist No. 46," January 29, 1788, Founders Online, National Archives, https://founders.archives.gov/documents/Madison/01-10-02-0261.

38 Patrick Henry, Virginia Debates on the Adoption of the Federal Constitution, June 9, 1788, Full text accessible through the Online Library of Liberty, https://oll.libertyfund.org/title/elliot-the-debates-in-the-several-state-conventions-vol-3.

39 Thomas Jefferson, Letter to Abigail Adams, February 22, 1787, Founders Online, National Archives, https://founders.archives.gov/documents/Adams/04-07-02-0187.

40 Thomas Jefferson, Letter to William Stephens Smith, November 13, 1787, Founders Online, National Archives, https://founders.archives.gov/documents/Jefferson/01-12-02-0348.

41 Thomas Jefferson, Letter to John Cartwright, June 5, 1824, Founders Online, National Archives, https://founders.archives.gov/documents/Jefferson/98-01-02-4313.

42 William Pitt, Parliamentary speech in the House of Commons, England, November 18, 1783, *The Speeches of the Right Honourable William Pitt in the House of Commons* (London: Longman, et al., 1806), 91, https://books.google.com/books?id=NC0BEvqsUOgC&printsec=frontcover&source=gbs_ge_summary_r&cad=0#v=onepage&q&f=false.

43 Daniel Webster, attributed to him in *The Beauties of the Hon. Daniel Webster*, ed. James Rees (New York: J. & H. G. Langley, 1839).

44 James Madison, "The Federalist No. 10," Founders Online, National Archives, https://founders.archives.gov/documents/Madison/01-10-02-0178.

45 Thomas Jefferson, *Notes on the State of Virginia*, Query XVII: Religion, 1781, Full text accessible through the University of Virginia, https://web.archive.org/web/2008 0914030942/http://etext.lib.virginia.edu/toc/modeng/public/JefVirg.html.

46 Thomas Paine, "The Rights of Man," Part 2, 1792, Full text accessible through the Gutenberg project at https://www.gutenberg.org/files/3742/3742-h/3742-h.htm#link2H_4_0008.

47 Richard Henry Lee, Letter to Samuel Adams, March 14, 1785, Full text accessible through the University of Chicago, https:// press-pubs.uchicago.edu/founders/documents/v1ch5s8.html.

48 James Madison, "Bounty Payments for Cod Fisheries," February 6, 1792, Founders Online, National Archives, https://founders. archives.gov/documents/Madison/01-14-02-0192.

49 John Adams, "To the Inhabitants of the Colony of Massachusetts-Bay," February 6, 1775, Founders Online, National Archives, https:// founders.archives.gov/documents/Adams/06-02-02-0072-0004.

50 Thomas Jefferson, Letter to C. Hammond, August 18, 1821, Founders Online, National Archives, https://founders. archives.gov/documents/Jefferson/03-17-02-0379.

51 Madison, "Bounty Payments," 1792.

52 John Locke, *Second Treatise of Government* (1690), Full text accessible through the Gutenberg Project, https://www. gutenberg.org/files/7370/7370-h/7370-h.htm.

53 John Adams, "A Dissertation on the Canon and Feudal Law," No. 4, October 21, 1765, Founders Online, National Archives, https:// founders.archives.gov/documents/Adams/06-01-02-0052-0007.

54 John Adams, "To the Inhabitants of the Colony of Massachusetts-Bay, January 23, 1775, Founders Online, National Archives, https:// founders.archives.gov/documents/Adams/06-02-02-0072-0002.

55 Thomas Jefferson, Letter to John Taylor, November 26, 1798, Founders Online, National Archives, https://founders.archives.gov/documents/ Jefferson/01-30-02-0398.
Letter to John Taylor, May 28, 1816, Founders Online, National Archives, https://founders.archives.gov/documents/ Jefferson/03-10-02-0053. The last sentence is from this later letter to Mr. Taylor. "Benevolence" has been used in placed of "funding."

56 Thomas Jefferson, Letter to James Madison, September 6, 1789, Founders Online, National Archives, https://founders. archives.gov/documents/Madison/01-12-02-0248.

57 Thomas Jefferson, Letter to Antoine Louis Claude Destutt de Tracy, December 26, 1820, Thomas Jefferson Foundation, https://tjrs.monticello.org/letter/1448.

58 George Washington, 5th Annual Address to Congress, December 3, 1793, Full text accessible through The American Presidency Project, University of California, https://www.presidency. ucsb.edu/documents/fifth-annual-address-congress.

59 Alexander Hamilton, "Fact No. 1," September 11, 1792, Founders Online, National Archives, https://founders.archives.gov/documents/ Hamilton/01-12-02-0274. Hamilton was quoting from his own report, "Report Relative to the Additional Supplies for the Ensuing Year, March 16, 1792.

60 Alexander Hamilton, "The Defence of the Funding System," July 1795, Founders Online, National Archives, https://founders. archives.gov/documents/Hamilton/01-19-02-0001.

61 George Washington, "Farewell Address," September 19, 1796, Founders Online, National Archives, https://founders.archives. gov/documents/Washington/05-20-02-0440-0002.

62 Benjamin Franklin, "Way to Wealth," 1758, Full text accessible at https:// archive.org/details/thewaytowealthbenjaminfranklin/page/n3/mode/2up.

63 Thomas Jefferson, Proposals to Revise the Virginia Constitution: I. Jefferson to "Henry Tompkinson" (Samuel Kercheval), July 12, 1816, Founders Online, National Archives, https://founders. archives.gov/documents/Jefferson/03-10-02-0128-0002.

64 Scribe, though the first mention of this quote appears to date back to a 1951 column by Elmer T. Peterson in the *Daily Oklahoman* who attributes it to Alexander Fraser Tytler.

65 Thomas Paine, *Common Sense* (Philadelphia: W. & T. Bradford, 1776), Full text accessible through the Gutenberg Project, https:// www.gutenberg.org/files/147/147-h/147-h.htm.

66 James Madison, "Madison Debates," Constitutional Convention, June 29, 1787, Avalon Project, Yale University, https://avalon.law.yale.edu/18th_century/ debates_629.asp.
Letter to Thomas Jefferson, May 13, 1798, Founders Online, National Archives, https://founders.archives.gov/documents/Madison/01-17-02-0088.

67 Thomas Jefferson, Letter to George Logan, November 12, 1816, Founders Online, National Archives, https://founders. archives.gov/documents/Jefferson/03-10-02-0390.

68 Booker T. Washington, *My Larger Education* (New York: Doubleday, Page, & Co., 1911), Full text accessible through the University of North Carolina, https://docsouth.unc.edu/fpn/washeducation/washing.html. In the original quote, Washington refers to a particular subset of African-Americans.

69 Washington, "Farewell Address," 1796.

70 James Madison, "The Federalist No. 10," November 22, 1787, Founders Online, National Archives, https://founders. archives.gov/documents/Madison/01-10-02-0178.

71 Madison, "No. 10," 1787.

72 Madison, "No. 10," 1787.

73 John Adams, VI. "A Dissertation on the Canon and the Feudal Law," No. 4, October 21, 1765, Founders Online, National Archives, https:// founders.archives.gov/documents/Adams/06-01-02-0052-0007.

74 James Madison, "Advice to My Country," December 1830, Founders Online, National Archives, https://founders. archives.gov/documents/Madison/99-02-02-2231.

75 John Adams, Letter to Richard Rush, May 14, 1821, Founders Online, National Archives, https://founders.archives.gov/documents/Adams/99-02-02-7491.

76 John Stuart Mill, Inaugural Address at the University of St. Andrews, February 1, 1867, https://babel.hathitrust.org/cgi/ pt?id=hvd.32044018937722&view=1up&seq=31&skin=2021.

CHAPTER EIGHT
PROPERTY

1 James Madison, "Import Duties, House of Representatives, April 9, 1789, Full text accessible through the University of Chicago, The Founders' Constitution, 2:1:8:1:18, https://press-pubs. uchicago.edu/founders/documents/a1_8_1s18.html.

2 Adam Smith, *An Inquiry into the Nature and Causes of the Wealth of Nations* (London, 1776), Full text accessible at https://www. gutenberg.org/files/3300/3300-h/3300-h.htm#chap01.

3 Smith, *Wealth of Nations*, 1776.

4 Smith, *Wealth of Nations*, 1776.

5   Smith, *Wealth of Nations*, 1776. While not verbatim, this quote popularly attributed to Smith summarizes the expressed sentiment found in this document.

6   Abraham Lincoln, Address before the Wisconsin State Agricultural Society, September 30, 1859, Full text accessible through https://teachingamericanhistory.org/document/address-before-the-wisconsin-state-agricultural-society/.

7   Roger Williams, Popularly credited to him, though our confidence is low despite no other mainline suggested attributions.

8   Alexander Hamilton, "The Federalist No. 12," November 27, 1787, Founders Online, National Archives, https://founders.archives.gov/documents/Hamilton/01-04-02-0165.

9   George Washington, Letter to Benjamin Harrison, October 10, 1784, Founders Online, National Archives, https://founders.archives.gov/documents/Washington/04-02-02-0082.

10   Thomas Jefferson, Letter to Martha Jefferson, March 28, 1787, Founders Online, National Archives, https://founders.archives.gov/documents/Jefferson/01-11-02-0244.

11   Alexander Hamilton, quoted in *Useful Information* by J. C. Thomas (Chicago: The Werner Co., 1895), https://books.google.com/books?id=AG5CAAAAIAAJ&q=alexander+hamilton#v=snippet&q=alexander%20hamilton&f=false. A friend of Hamilton's claimed that Hamilton said this.

12   Frederick Douglass, "Self-Made Men," delivered in 1872, Full text accessible through Monadnock Valley Press, https://monadnock.net/douglass/self-made-men.html.

13   Booker T. Washington, *Up From Slavery: An Autobiography* (New York: Doubleday, Page, & Co., 1901), Full text accessible through the Gutenberg Project, https://www.gutenberg.org/files/2376/2376-h/2376-h.htm.

14   W. E. B. Dubois, popularly attributed to *The Souls of Black Folk* (Chicago: A. C. McClurg, & Co., 1903), Full text accessible through the Gutenberg Project, https://www.gutenberg.org/files/408/408-h/408-h.htm.

15   Henry Clay, popularly attributed with a slightly lower confidence as the primary source could not be located, https://www.azquotes.com/quote/1056564.

16   Ralph Waldo Emerson, Lecture delivered to the Mechanics' Apprentices' Library Association in Boston, January 25, 1841, Full text accessible through Virginia Commonwealth University, https://archive.vcu.edu/english/engweb/transcendentalism/authors/emerson/essays/manreform.html.

17   Henry David Thoreau, *Walden* (Concord, MA, 1854), Full
     text accessible through the Gutenberg Project, https://www.
     gutenberg.org/files/205/205-h/205-h.htm#chap02.

18   Smith, *Wealth of Nations*, 1776.

19   John Locke, *Second Treatise of Government* (1690), Full text
     accessible through the Gutenberg Project, https://www.
     gutenberg.org/files/7370/7370-h/7370-h.htm.

20   Smith, *Wealth of Nations*, 1776.

21   Locke, *Second Treatise*, 1690.

22   Thomas Jefferson, "First Inaugural Address," March 4, 1801,
     Founders Online, National Archives, https://founders.archives.
     gov/documents/Jefferson/01-33-02-0116-0004.

23   James Madison, "Property," *National Gazette*, March 27,
     1792, Founders Online, National Archives, https://founders.
     archives.gov/documents/Madison/01-14-02-0238.

24   Ralph Waldo Emerson, "Politics," *Essays* (Second Series,
     1844), Full text accessible through Virginia Commonwealth
     University, https://archive.vcu.edu/english/engweb/
     transcendentalism/authors/emerson/essays/politics.html.

25   Thomas Jefferson, Letter to Samuel Kercheval ("Henry Tompkinson"),
     July 12, 1816, Founders Online, National Archives, https://founders.
     archives.gov/documents/Jefferson/03-10-02-0128-0002.

26   John Dickinson, "Letters from a Farmer in Pennsylvania to the
     Inhabitants of the British Colonies," *Pennsylvania Chronicle*, November 30—
     December 3, 1767, Full text accessible through the Gutenberg Project,
     https://www.gutenberg.org/files/47111/47111-h/47111-h.htm.

27   John Adams, "A Defence of the Constitutions of Government of the United
     States," 1787, *The Founders' Constitution* 1:16:15, University of Chicago,
     https://press-pubs.uchicago.edu/founders/documents/v1ch16s15.html.

28   Frederic Bastiat, "The Law," (1850), McMaster University, https://
     socialsciences.mcmaster.ca/econ/ugcm/3ll3/bastiat/TheLaw.htm. This
     a quotation inlaid in another quotation from the same work. The second
     conditional clause stems from a section on identifying legal plunder, while the
     rest of the quotation is derived from a section concerning the law and charity.

29   John Adams, *A Defense of the Constitution of Government of the United States* (1787), vol. 1, Full text accessible through the Online Library of Liberty, https://oll.libertyfund.org/title/adams-the-works-of-john-adams-vol-4.

30   David Hume, "An Enquiry Concerning the Principles of Morals," 1777, Full text accessible through the Gutenberg Project, https://www.gutenberg.org/files/4320/4320-h/4320-h.htm.

31   Alexis de Tocqueville, *Democracy in America*, vol. 2, trans. by Henry Reeve, Full text through Gutenberg Project, https://www.gutenberg.org/files/816/816-h/816-h.htm.

32   Samuel Adams, "House of Representatives of Massachusetts to Dennys De Berdt," January 12, 1768, Full text accessible through the University of Chicago, https://press-pubs.uchicago.edu/founders/documents/v1ch16s6.html.

33   James Madison, *Philadelphia Gazette,* January 14, 1794, Founders Online, National Archives, https://founders.archives.gov/documents/Madison/01-15-02-0117. This was reported of Madison by the newspaper.

34   Frederic Bastiat, "Economic Sophisms," 1845, Full text accessible through the Online Library of Liberty, http://files.libertyfund.org/files/276/Bastiat_0182_EBk_v6.0.pdf.

35   Frederic Bastiat, "The Law," (1850), McMaster University, https://socialsciences.mcmaster.ca/econ/ugcm/3ll3/bastiat/TheLaw.htm.

36   Friedrich Nietzsche, *The Will to Power*, vol. I-II, translated by Anthony M. Ludovici (Edinburgh: T.N. Foulis, 1914), Full text accessible through the Gutenberg Project, https://www.gutenberg.org/files/52914/52914-h/52914-h.htm and https://www.gutenberg.org/files/52915/52915-h/52915-h.htm.

37   Bastiat, "Law," 1850.

38   Thomas Jefferson, Letter to Thomas Cooper, November 29, 1802, Founders Online, National Archives, https://founders.archives.gov/documents/Jefferson/01-39-02-0070. First sentence comes from this work. Editorial note on a Prospectus for Destutt de Tracy's *Treatise on Political Economy*, including in a letter to Joseph Milligan, April 6, 1816, Full text accessible through the Claremont Institute, https://founding.com/founders-library/american-political-figures/thomas-jefferson/letter-to-joseph-milligan/. The second sentence in the quotation comes from this work; Jefferson places the last clause in quotes.

39   Abraham Lincoln, Letter to New York Workingmen's Democratic
Republican Association, March 21, 1864, from *Collected Works of
Abraham Lincoln*, vol. 7, University of Michigan, https://quod.lib.
umich.edu/l/lincoln/lincoln7/1:566?rgn=div1;view=fulltext.

40   John Adams, Letter to Thomas Jefferson, August 25, 1787,
Founders Online, National Archives, https ://founders.
archives.gov/documents/Jefferson/01-12-02-0064.

41   Benjamin Franklin, "'Arator': On the Price of Corn, & Management
of the Poor," November 29, 1766, Founders Online, National Archives,
https://founders.archives.gov/documents/Franklin/01-13-02-0194.

42   Frederick Douglass, "What Shall Be Done with the Slaves If Emancipated?"
Douglass' Monthly, January, 1862, Full text accessible through the
University of Rochester, https://rbscp.lib.rochester.edu/4386.

43   Franklin, "'Arator'," 1766.

44   Thomas Jefferson, *Notes on the State of Virginia* (Philadelphia: Prichard
& Hall, 1788), Full text accessible through the University of North
Carolina, https://docsouth.unc.edu/southlit/jefferson/jefferson.html.

45   Franklin, "'Arator'," 1766.

46   Harriet Tubman, quoted in *Scenes in the Life of Harriet Tubman*
by Sarah H. Bradford (Auburn: W. J. Moses, 1869), Full text
accessible through the Gutenberg Project, https://www.
gutenberg.org/files/57821/57821-h/57821-h.htm.

47   Booker T. Washington, *Up From Slavery: An Autobiography* (New York:
Doubleday, Page, & Co., 1901), Full text accessible through the Gutenberg
Project, https://www.gutenberg.org/files/2376/2376-h/2376-h.htm.

48   Thomas Jefferson, Letter to Jose Correa da Serra, November 25, 1817,
Founders Online, National Archives, https://founders.archives.gov/
documents/Jefferson/03-12-02-0166. First half of the quotation is from this
work.
"Report of the Board of Commissioners for the University of Virginia to
the Virginia General Assembly, August 4, 1818, Founders Online, National
Archives, https://founders.archives.gov/documents/Madison/04-01-02-0289.

49   John Hancock, as quoted in *Forbes*, https://www.
forbes.com/?sh=2b342e212254.

50   Rev. William J. H. Boetcker, "The Ten Cannots," https://
www.appleseeds.org//10_Cannots.htm.

[51]   Henry Ward Beecher, *Life Thoughts* (Boston: Phillips, Sampson, & Co., 1859), full text accessible through University of Michigan, https://quod.lib.umich.edu/cgi/t/text/text-idx?c=moa;idno=AJK2188. While not verbatim, this quote has been updated with modern language to express the sentiment found in Beecher's writings.

[52]   Booker T. Washington, "Democracy and Education," Delivered at the Institute of Arts & Sciences in Brooklyn, New York, September 30, 1896, https://www.blackpast.org/african-american-history/speeches-african-american-history/1896-booker-t-washington-democracy-and-education/.

CHAPTER NINE
LAW

[1]   Alexander Hamilton, "Tully No. III," *The American Daily* Advertiser, August 28, 1794, Founders Online, National Archives, https://founders.archives.gov/documents/Hamilton/01-17-02-0130.

[2]   John Locke, *Second Treatise of Government* (1690), Full text accessible through the Gutenberg Project, https://www.gutenberg.org/files/7370/7370-h/7370-h.htm.

[3]   Benjamin Rush, Letter to David Ramsay, 1748, *Letters of Benjamin Rush*, vol. 1, ed. Lyman Henry Butterfield (Princeton, 1951), 454.

[4]   Frederick Douglass, "The Present and Future of the Colored Race in America," June 1863, Full text accessible through Teaching American History, https://teachingamericanhistory.org/document/the-present-and-future-of-the-colored-race-in-america/.

[5]   Anna Cooper, "Woman Versus the Indian," *Voice from the South* (Xenia, OH: The Aldine Printing House, 1892), 120-121, Full text accessible through the University of North Carolina, https://docsouth.unc.edu/church/cooper/cooper.html#coope80.

[6]   Theodore Weld, Letter to William Lloyd Garrison, January 2, 1833, Digital Commonwealth, https://www.digitalcommonwealth.org/search/commonwealth:2z10zh817. Within the narrow context of the correspondence, "Society" referred to the New England Anti-Slavery Society, though the wider context used is still applicable.

[7]   Alexander Hamilton, Constitutional Convention Remarks on Equality of Representation of the States in the Congress, June 29, 1787, Founders Online, National Archives, https://founders.archives.gov/documents/Hamilton/01-04-02-0109.

[8] John Jay, "The State of Georgia v. Brailsford, et al.", U. S. Supreme Court, February 7, 1794, Full text accessible through Cornell University, https://www.law.cornell.edu/supremecourt/text/3/1.

[9] Weld, Letter to Garrison, 1833.

[10] George Mason, "The Virginia Declaration of Rights," June 12, 1776, America's Founding Documents, National Archives, https://www.archives.gov/founding-docs/virginia-declaration-of-rights.

[11] Benjamin Franklin, "Emblematical Representation," *The Works of Benjamin Franklin: Containing Several Political & Historical Tracts Not Included in Any Former Edition and Many Letters Official and Private Not Hitherto Published*, vol. 4, ed. Jared Sparks (Boston: Hilliard, Gray, & Co., 1837), 457.

[12] The Constitution of the United States: A Transcription, America's Founding Documents, National Archives, https://www.archives.gov/founding-docs/constitution-transcript.

[13] Frederick Douglass, "Southern Barbarism," delivered in Washington, D.C., April 16, 1886 on the occasion of the 24th anniversary of the Emancipation, Full text accessible on https://dex.tumblr.com/post/95420751031/southern-barbarism-by-frederick-douglass.

[14] Hamilton, "Tully No. III," 1794.

[15] Thomas Jefferson, Letter to Adamantios Coray, October 31, 1823, Founders Online, National Archives, https://founders.archives.gov/documents/Jefferson/98-01-02-3837.

[16] James Monroe, Virginia Constitutional Convention, June 10, 1788, *Famous American Statesmen & Orators*, vol. 2, ed. Alexander K. McClure (New York: F. F. Lovell, 1902), 33.

[17] Frederic Bastiat, "The Law," (1850), McMaster University, https://socialsciences.mcmaster.ca/econ/ugcm/3ll3/bastiat/TheLaw.htm. "Fallacy" has replaced "prejudice;" "seductive lure" for "fascinating side."

[18] Bastiat, "The Law," 1850.

[19] Bastiat, "The Law," 1850.

[20] George Washington, Fragments of the Discarded First Inaugural Address, April, 1789, https://teachingamericanhistory.org/document/fragments-of-the-discarded-first-inaugural-address/.

21 John Adams, "VII. An Essay on Man's Lust for Power,"
    Founders Online, National Archives, https://founders.archives.
    gov/documents/Adams/06-01-02-0045-0008.

22 Abraham Lincoln, "The Perpetuation of Our Political Institutions," delivered
    on January 27, 1838, to the Young Men's Lyceum of Springfield, IL, Full
    text accessible through the University of Michigan, https://quod.lib.umich.
    edu/j/jala/2629860.0006.103/--perpetuation-of-our-political-institutions-add
    ress?rgn=main;view=fulltext.

23 Lincoln, "Lyceum," 1838.

24 Joseph Story, *Commentaries on the Constitution of the United
    States*, 2nd ed., vol. 2, chapter XLV (1851), 617, as cited by
    Bartleby, https://www.bartleby.com/73/63.html.

25 Samuel Adams, unsigned letter printed in the Boston Gazette, April 2,
    1781, included in *The Writings of Samuel Adams*, ed. Harry Alonzo Cushing,
    vol. 4, 1778-1802 (New York: G. P. Putnam's Sons, 1908), 253.

26 Viscount Bolingbroke, "The Occasional Writer, No. 3,"
    February 13, 1726-7, *The Works of Henry St. John, Lord Viscount
    Bolingbroke*, vol. 1 (London: J. Johnson, et al., 1809), 235.

27 James Madison, "The Federalist No. 62," February 27,
    1788, Founders Online, National Archives, https://founders.
    archives.gov/documents/Hamilton/01-04-02-0212.

28 Madison, "Federalist 62," 1788.

29 Madison, "Federalist 62," 1788.

30 John Marshall, William Marbury v. James Madison," U. S. Supreme
    Court, February term, 1803, Full text accessible through Cornell
    University, https://www.law.cornell.edu/supremecourt/text/5/137.

31 Marshall, "Marbury v. Madison," 1803.

32 Marshall, "Marbury v. Madison," 1803.

33 Hamilton, "Tully No. III," 1794.

34 Abraham Lincoln, "House Divided Speech," Illinois Republican
    State Convention, June 16, 1858, Springfield, IL, Full text
    accessible through the National Park Service, https://www.
    nps.gov/liho/learn/historyculture/housedivided.htm.

[35] George Washington, Letter to James Madison, November 30, 1785, Founders Online, National Archives, https://founders.archives.gov/GEWN-04-03-02-0357.

[36] William Lloyd Garrison, Open Letter to the Public, *The Liberator*, January 1, 1831, Full text accessible through the Public Broadcasting Station, https://www.pbs.org/wgbh/aia/part4/4h2928t.html.

[37] John Locke, "An Essay Concerning Human Understanding," (London: Eliz. Holt, 1690), Full text accessible through the Gutenberg Project, https://www.gutenberg.org/files/10615/10615-h/10615-h.htm.

[38] Thomas Jefferson, Letter to Henry Lee, August 10, 1824, Founders Online, National Archives, https://founders.archives.gov/documents/Jefferson/98-01-02-4451. This quote may be sourced to a 1980 tract on regulation which appears to have condensed the sentiments Jefferson expressed in his letter to Lee.

[39] Thomas Jefferson, Draft Declaration and Protest of Virginia, December 1825, Full text accessible through the Avalon Project, Yale University, https://avalon.law.yale.edu/19th_century/jeffdec1.asp.

[40] George Washington, Letter to Henry Lee, Jr., October 31, 1786, Founders Online, National Archives, https://founders.archives.gov/documents/Washington/04-04-02-0286.

[41] Thomas Jefferson, Letter to James Monroe, June 17, 1785, Founders Online, National Archives, https://founders.archives.gov/documents/Jefferson/01-08-02-0174.

[42] Thomas Jefferson, Letter to William Stephens Smith, February 2, 1788, Founders Online, National Archives, https://founders.archives.gov/documents/Jefferson/01-12-02-0590.

[43] George Washington, Letter to the States, June 8, 1783, Founders Online, National Archives, https://founders.archives.gov/documents/Washington/99-01-02-11404.

[44] Myron Magnet, "The Vision of the Founding Fathers," July 3, 2015, *National Review*, https://www.nationalreview.com/2015/07/vision-founding-fathers/. While attributed to Scribe, this quotation is from Mr. Magnet.

[45] Samuel Adams, Letter to James Warren, October 24, 1780, "Revolutionary War and Beyond," https://www.revolutionary-war-and-beyond.com/Samuel-Adams-Letter-24Oct1780.html.

46   Samuel Adams, The Report of the Committee of Correspondence
      to the Boston Town Meeting, November 20, 1772, The Rights of
      the Colonists, https://history.hanover.edu/texts/adamss.html.

47   Samuel Adams, Essay in *The Boston Gazette*, October 14, 1771,
      "Revolutionary War and Beyond," https://www.revolutionary-
      war-and-beyond.com/samuel-adams-quotes-1.html.

48   Scribe. See Note 44 for quote from Myron Magnet.

49   Roger Sherman, "What True Patriotism Demands of the American
      Citizen," *The American Magazine of Civics*, ed. Andrew Palm &
      Henry R. Waite, vol. 6 (New York: Palm, 1895), 398.

50   John Adams, Letter to Abigail Adams, July 7, 1775, Founders Online, National
      Archives, https://founders.archives.gov/documents/Adams/04-01-02-0160.

51   Daniel Webster. This quotation is a paraphrasing of several separate
      quotations from Webster. The following link has researched and divided
      up this quotation to give the reader context and information for each
      portion, https://en.wikiquote.org/wiki/Talk:Daniel_Webster.

Chapter Ten
Call

1   Abraham Lincoln, "The Perpetuation of Our Political Institutions," delivered
     on January 27, 1838, to the Young Men's Lyceum of Springfield, IL, Full
     text accessible through the University of Michigan, https://quod.lib.umich.
     edu/j/jala/2629860.0006.103/--perpetuation-of-our-political-institutions-add
     ress?rgn=main;view=fulltext.

2   Lincoln, "Lyceum," 1838. See notes.

3   Montesquieu, *The Spirit of the Laws* (1748), Book VIII, Ch. 1, Full text accessible
     through the Online Library of Liberty, https://oll.libertyfund.org/title/
     montesquieu-complete-works-vol-1-the-spirit-of-laws. The original quote is: The
     corruption of each government generally begins with that of the principles.

4   Samuel Adams, speech delivered at the State House in Philadelphia,
     August 1, 1776, Abridged version accessible through the National Center
     for Public Policy, https://nationalcenter.org/ncppr/2001/11/03/
     samuel-adams-advocates-american-independence-1776/.

5   Thomas Jefferson, Extract and Commentary printed in the New York
     Minerva, May 2, 1797, Founders Online, National Archives, https://
     founders.archives.gov/documents/Jefferson/01-29-02-0054-0004.

6   Alexis de Tocqueville, *Democracy in America*, vol. 2, trans. by
    Henry Reeve, Full text through Gutenberg Project, https://
    www.gutenberg.org/files/816/816-h/816-h.htm.

7   Patrick Henry, "Give Me Liberty or Give Me Death," March 23,
    1775, Full text accessible through the Avalon Project, Yale University,
    https://avalon.law.yale.edu/18th_century/patrick.asp.

8   Henry, "Liberty or Death," 1775.

9   Alexander Hamilton, "The Federalist No. 33," January 2,
    1788, Founders Online, National Archives, https://founders.
    archives.gov/documents/Hamilton/01-04-02-0190.

10 Abraham Lincoln, included in his notes for speeches delivered in
    the latter part of 1859, as documented by the Library of Congress'
    "Abraham Lincoln Papers," https://www.loc.gov/item/mal0189300/.

11 "Declaration of Independence," U.S. Congress, July 4, 1776, National
    Archives, https://www.archives.gov/founding-docs/declaration-transcript.

12 Thomas Jefferson, enclosed proposal for the state of Virginia in a letter to
    James Madison, December 24, 1825, Founders Online, National Archives,
    https://founders.archives.gov/documents/Madison/04-03-02-0679.

13 Mercy Otis Warren, *The Rise, Progress, and Termination of the American Revolution*,
    vol. 3, (Boston: Manning & Loring, 1805), 414, https://play.google.com/store/
    books/details?id=hB0wAAAAYAAJ&rdid=book-hB0wAAAAYAAJ&rdot=1.

14 James Madison, "The Federalist No. 41," January 19, 1788,
    Founders Online, National Archives, https://founders.
    archives.gov/documents/Madison/01-10-02-0237.

15 Abraham Lincoln, Address to the 166th Ohio Regiment, August 22,
    1864, Full text accessible through the National Park Service, https://
    www.nps.gov/liho/learn/historyculture/thankstotroops.htm.

16 Abraham Lincoln, Address to Congressional Representatives from the Border
    States, July 12, 1862, full text accessible through the University of Maryland,
    http://www.freedmen.umd.edu/bordstat.htm.
    Lincoln, "166th Ohio," 1864. The last two sentences are from this speech.

17 Daniel Webster, Public Reception in Madison, Indiana, June 1,
    1837, *The Works of Daniel Webster*, vol. 1 (Boston: Little, Brown, &
    Co., 1860), 404, https://play.google.com/store/books/details?id=
    KhQbAAAAIAAJ&rdid=book-KhQbAAAAIAAJ&rdot=1.

18   Thomas Paine, *The American Crisis,* #4. September 12, 1777, Full text accessible through the Gutenberg Project, https://www.gutenberg. org/files/3741/3741-h/3741-h.htm#link2H_4_0002.

19   George Mason, Letter to George Washington, April 5, 1769, ConSource, https://www.consource.org/document/ george-mason-to-george-washington-1769-4-5/.

20   Thomas Paine, *The American Crisis,* #1. December 23, 1776, Full text accessible through the Gutenberg Project, https://www.gutenberg. org/files/3741/3741-h/3741-h.htm#link2H_4_0002.

21   Samuel Adams, as Candidus in the *Boston Gazette,* October 14, 1771, Full text accessible through The Federalist Papers, https://thefederalistpapers.org/founders/samuel-adams/ samuel-adams-writing-as-candidus-essay-in-the-boston-gazette-oct-14-1771.

22   James Otis, "Against the Writs of Assistance," February 24, 1761, Full text accessible through the University of Pennsylvania, https://www. sas.upenn.edu/~cavitch/pdf-library/Otis_Against%20Writs.pdf.

23   Samuel Adams, speech delivered at the State House in Philadelphia, August 1, 1776, Abridged version accessible through the National Center for Public Policy, https://nationalcenter.org/ncppr/2001/11/03/ samuel-adams-advocates-american-independence-1776/.

24   Paine, *Crisis,* #1., 1776.

25   S. Adams, Philadelphia speech, 1776.

26   Paine, *Crisis,* #1., 1776.

27   John Adams, Letter to Abigail Adams, April 26, 1777, Founders Online, National Archives, https://founders. archives.gov/documents/Adams/04-02-02-0169.

28   Adams, Letter to Abigail, 1777.

29   Benjamin Franklin, Pennsylvania Assembly: Reply to the Governor, November 11, 1755, Founders Online, National Archives, https:// founders.archives.gov/documents/Franklin/01-06-02-0107.

30   Thomas Jefferson, Letter to James Madison, January 30, 1787, Founders Online, National Archives, https://founders.archives.gov/documents/ Jefferson/01-11-02-0095. Jefferson quoted the Latin saying in its original language: *Malo periculosam, libertatem quam quietam servitutem.*

31 Thomas Jefferson, Letter to Philip Mazzei, April 24, 1796, Founders Online, National Archives, https://founders.archives.gov/documents/Jefferson/01-29-02-0054-0002. "Eternal vigilance," a popular phrase in the 19th century, has been substituted for "unremitting labors and perils."

32 Paine, *Crisis*, #1., 1776.

33 Henry, "Liberty or Death," 1775.

34 Henry, "Liberty or Death," 1775.

35 Patrick Henry, *The Debates in the Several State Conventions on the Adoption of the Federal Constitution*, vol. 3, ed. Jonathan Elliot, (Washington, D.C.: 1836).

36 John Adams, "A Dissertation on the Canon and the Feudal Law," No. 3, September 30, 1765, Founders Online, National Archives, https://founders.archives.gov/documents/Adams/06-01-02-0052-0006.

37 John Adams, *The Greatest Speeches of the Defender of the Constitution*, Daniel Webster (Boston: Little, Brown, and Co., 1907), 93-96. Webster describes the speech as the "supposed speech of John Adams in favor of the Declaration."

38 Nathan Hale, last words before being hanged by the British as a spy, as captured by Capt. John Montresor and conveyed to William Hull, https://en.wikiquote.org/wiki/Nathan_Hale.

39 John Hancock, Boston Massacre Oration, March 5, 1774, Full text accessible through Monticello.org, https://classroom.monticello.org/view/73271/.

40 Hancock, Boston, 1774.

41 George Washington, Letter to George Mason, March 27, 1779, Founders Online, National Archives, https://founders.archives.gov/documents/Washington/03-19-02-0609.

42 Abraham Lincoln, Annual Message to Congress, December 1, 1862, https://www.abrahamlincolnonline.org/lincoln/speeches/congress.htm.

43 Abraham Lincoln, "Gettysburg Address," November 19, 1863, Our Documents, https://www.ourdocuments.gov/doc.php?flash=false&doc=36&page=transcript.

44 William Lloyd Garrison, "No Compromise with the Evils of Slavery," speech delivered in 1854, Civil Rights and Conflict in the United States: Selected Speeches, USF, https://etc.usf.edu/lit2go/185/civil-rights-and-conflict-in-the-united-states-selected-speeches/5061/no-compromise-with-the-evil-of-slavery-speech-1854/.

BIBLIOGRAPHY

This abbreviated bibliography has been particularly assembled for the specific purpose of serving as a launchpad of sorts for those who desire to learn more about the Founding Fathers and related minds. It reflects many of the primary sources consulted for this book. Surprisingly, much of the text in *The Founders' Speech* originates from their private correspondence. Some of the most cherished words from Presidents Thomas Jefferson and John Adams, for example, came from their personal letters back and forth throughout the years. Aside from these treasures (which serve as ample fodder for intellectual rabbit trails), many distinguished classics have been included as well; while familiar with many Americans, they remain largely unread to our detriment. By the nature of their age and eminence, most of these materials can be accessed in full online. Where this is not the case, additional information has been provided.

Adams, Abigail and John Adams. *Familiar Letters of John Adams and His Wife Abigail Adams, During the Revolution.* Ed. Charles Francis Adams. New York: Hurd & Houghton, 1875. Text accessible through the Gutenberg Project, https://www.gutenberg.org/files/34123/34123-h/34123-h.htm.

———, and Thomas Jefferson. *The Adams-Jefferson Letters.* Ed. Lester J. Cappon. Chapel Hill, NC: The University of North Carolina Press, 1959. Their correspondence can also be accessed online through the National Archives, https://founders.archives.gov/.

Adams, John. *A Defence of the Constitutions of Government of the United States of America.* 3 vols. London: Charles Dilly, 1787-1788. Text accessible through the Online Library of Liberty's 10-volume collection on the works of John Adams, https://oll.libertyfund.org/title/adams-the-works-of-john-adams-10-vols.

————. "A Dissertation on the Canon and Feudal Law." No. 1-4. *Boston Gazette*, August 12–October 21, 1765. Founders Online, National Archives, https://founders.archives.gov/?q=Project%3A%22Adams%20Papers%22%20Period%3A%22Colonial%22%20Recipient%3A%22Boston%20Gazette%20%28newspaper%29%22&s=1511211111&r=1.

————. "The Papers of John Adams." Founders Online, National Archives, https://founders.archives.gov/. This website contains over 10,000 of Adams' documents, including his private correspondence.

————. *The Works of John Adams*. 10 vols. Ed. Charles Francis Adams. Boston: Little, Brown, & Co., 1856. Text accessible through the Online Library of Liberty, https://oll.libertyfund.org/title/adams-the-works-of-john-adams-10-vols.

Adams, Samuel. "Famous Documents and Speeches." Samuel Adams Heritage Society, http://www.samuel-adams-heritage.com/documents-and-speeches.html. The speech concerning the Declaration of Independence is highly recommended.

————. *The Writings of Samuel Adams*. 4 vols. Ed. Harry Alonzo Cushing. New York: G. P. Putnam's Sons, 1904. Text accessible through archive.org, https://archive.org/search.php?query=The%20Writings%20of%20Samuel%20Adams%20Harry%20Alonzo%20Cushing.

"The Anti-Federalist Papers." Ed. Morton Borden East Lansing, MI: Michigan State University Press, 1965. Text accessible through the University of Tulsa, http://resources.utulsa.edu/law/classes/rice/Constitutional/AntiFederalist/antifed.htm.

Bastiat, Frederic. *La Loi*. Paris: Guillaumin, 1850. Translated text of *The Law* accessible through McMaster University, https://socialsciences.mcmaster.ca/econ/ugcm/3ll3/bastiat/TheLaw.htm.

"The Bill of Rights." National Archives, https://www.archives.gov/founding-docs/bill-of-rights-transcript.

"The Constitution." National Archives, https://www.archives.gov/founding-docs/constitution-transcript.

"Declaration of Independence." National Archives, https://www.archives.gov/founding-docs/declaration-transcript.

Douglass, Frederick. *Narrative of the Life of Frederick Douglass*. Boston: The Anti-Slavery Office, 1845. Text accessible through the Gutenberg Project, https://www.gutenberg.org/files/23/23-h/23-h.htm.

Dubois, W. E. B. *The Souls of Black Folk*. Chicago: A. C. McClurg, & Co., 1903. Text accessible through the Gutenberg Project, https://www.gutenberg.org/files/408/408-h/408-h.htm.

"The Federalist Papers." Text accessible through the Library of Congress, https://guides.loc.gov/federalist-papers/full-text.

Franklin, Benjamin. *Autobiography of Benjamin Franklin*. New York: Henry Holt & Co., 1916. Text accessible through the Gutenberg Project, https://www.gutenberg.org/files/20203/20203-h/20203-h.htm.

———. "Silence Dogood Letters." April 2–August 13, 1722. Founders Online, National Archives, https://founders.archives.gov/index.xqy?q=silence+dogood&s=1511211111&r=1.

———. *Way to Wealth*. 1758. Text accessible at https://archive.org/details/thewaytowealthbenjaminfranklin/page/n3/mode/2up.

Garrison, William Lloyd. "No Compromise with the Evils of Slavery." Speech, 1854. Text accessible through the University of South Florida, https://etc.usf.edu/lit-2go/185/civil-rights-and-conflict-in-the-united-states-selected-speeches/5061/no-compromise-with-the-evil-of-slavery-speech-1854/.

Hamilton, Alexander. *The Farmer Refuted*. February 23, 1775. Founders Online, National Archives, https://founders.archives.gov/documents/Hamilton/01-01-02-0057.

Henry, Patrick. "Give Me Liberty or Give Me Death." March 23, 1775. Text accessible through Yale University's Avalon Project, https://avalon.law.yale.edu/18th_century/patrick.asp.

———. Speech to Virginia Ratifying Convention. June 5, 1788. Text accessible through *Teaching American History*, https://teachingamericanhistory.org/document/patrickhenry-virginia-ratifying-convention-va/.

Jefferson, Thomas. "First Inaugural Address." March 4, 1801. Founders Online, National Archives, https://founders.archives.gov/documents/Jefferson/01-33-02-0116-0004.

———. *Notes on the State of Virginia*. Philadelphia: Pritchard & Hall, 1788. Text accessible through the University of North Carolina, https://docsouth.unc.edu/southlit/jefferson/jefferson.html.

———. *The Writings of Thomas Jefferson*. 9 vols. Ed. H. A. Washington. Washington, D.C.: Taylor & Maury, 1853–1854. Text accessible through the Hathitrust Digital Library, https://catalog.hathitrust.org/Record/000365325.

Lincoln, Abraham. *The Collected Works of Abraham Lincoln*. 8 vols. Ed. Roy P. Basler. New Brunswick, NJ: Rutgers University Press, 1953. Full text of all 8 volumes accessible through the University of Michigan, https://quod.lib.umich.edu/l/lincoln/.

———. "Gettysburg Address." November 19, 1863. Text accessible through Cornell University, https://rmc.library.cornell.edu/gettysburg/good_cause/transcript.htm.

———. Speech, Edwardsville, IL. September 11, 1858. Text accessible through the University of Michigan, https://quod.lib.umich.edu/l/lincoln/lincoln3/1:13?rgn=div1;view=fulltext.

Locke, John. *An Essay Concerning Humane Understanding*. 4 vols. London: Eliz. Holt, 1690. Text accessible through the Gutenberg Project, https://www.gutenberg.org/files/10615/10615-h/10615-h.htm.

――――. *Second Treatise of Government*. London, 1690. Text accessible through the Gutenberg Project, https://www.gutenberg.org/files/7370/7370-h/7370-h.htm.

Mill, John Stuart. *On Liberty*. London: Walter Scott Publishing Co., 1901. Text accessible through the Gutenberg Project, https://www.gutenberg.org/files/34901/34901-h/34901-h.htm.

Paine, Thomas. *The Writings of Thomas Paine*. vol. 1, 1774–1779: The American Crisis. Ed. Moncure Daniel Conway. Text accessible through the Gutenberg Project, https://www.gutenberg.org/files/3741/3741-h/3741-h.htm.

――――. *Common Sense*. Philadelphia: W. & T. Bradford, 1776. Text accessible through the Gutenberg Project, https://www.gutenberg.org/files/147/147-h/147-h.htm.

Smith, Adam. *An Inquiry into the Nature and Causes of the Wealth of Nations*. London: 1776. Text accessible through the Gutenberg Project, https://www.gutenberg.org/files/3300/3300-h/3300-h.htm#chap01.

――――. "The Theory of Moral Sentiments." *The Essays of Adam Smith*. London: Alex Murray & Co., 1872. Text accessible through the University of Michigan, https://www.gutenberg.org/files/58559/58559-h/58559-h.htm.

de Tocqueville, Alexis. *Democracy in America*. 2 vols. 1835, 1840. Trans. by Henry Reeve. Text accessible through the Gutenberg Project, https://www.gutenberg.org/files/816/816-h/816-h.htm.

Washington, George. "Farewell Address." September 19, 1796. Founders Online, National Archives, https://founders.archives.gov/documents/Washington/05-20-02-0440-0002.

――――. "First Inaugural Address." April 30, 1789, Founders Online, National Archives, https://www.archives.gov/exhibits/american_originals/inaugtxt.html.

――――. *The Writings of George Washington*. 14 vols. Ed. Worthington Chauncey Ford. New York: G. P. Putnam's Sons, 1889–1893. Text accessible through the Online Library of Liberty, https://oll.libertyfund.org//title/ford-the-writings-of-george-washington-14-vols.

Washington, Booker T. *Up From Slavery: An Autobiography*. New York: Doubleday, Page, & Co., 1901. Text accessible through the Gutenberg Project, https://www.gutenberg.org/files/2376/2376-h/2376-h.htm.

Webster, Daniel. *Daniel Webster for Young Americans*. Boston: Little, Brown, & Co., 1907. Text accessible through the Gutenberg Project, https://www.gutenberg.org/files/41300/41300-h/41300-h.htm.

BIBLIOGRAPHY

Webster, Noah. *A Collection of Essays and Fugitiv Writings* [sic]. Boston: I. Thomas & E. T. Andrews, 1790. Text accessible through the Gutenberg Project, https://www.gutenberg.org/files/44416/44416-h/44416-h.htm.

THE GREAT SEAL OF THE
UNITED STATES

Before adjourning on July 4, 1776, the Continental Congress passed the following resolution:

"Resolved, that Dr. Franklin, Mr. J. Adams, and Mr. Jefferson, be a committee, to bring in a device for a seal for the United States of America."

These illustrious Founders proposed several fascinating preliminary concepts for a seal to represent the new nation, drawing on classical and biblical imagery. In an August 14, 1776 letter to his wife Abigail, John Adams recounted some of the debate. Benjamin Franklin, Adams wrote, suggested "Moses lifting up his wand, and dividing the Red Sea, and Pharoah, in his chariot overwhelmed with the waters," and the following motto, "Rebellion to tyrants is obedience to God." Thomas Jefferson imagined Americans as "the children of Israel in the wilderness...led by a pillar of fire by night," alongside representations of early Britons "whose political principles and form of government" the United States assumed. Adams concentrated on Hercules, the mythical figure of strength, "resting on his club," gazing towards a figure of virtue, and impervious to sloth and vice.

In 1782, after six years and three committees, the Continental Congress decided on a less abstract seal and incorporated a design that reflected the beliefs and values that the Founding Fathers ascribed to the new nation. Charles Thomson, Secretary of the Continental Congress, designed the 1782 seal to symbolize our country's strength, unity, and independence. The **olive branch** and the **arrows** held in the eagle's talons denote the power of peace and war. The **eagle** always casts its gaze toward the olive branch signifying that our nation desires to pursue peace but stands ready to defend itself. The **shield**, or escutcheon, is "born on the breast of an American Eagle without any other supporters to denote that the United States of America ought to rely on their own Virtue," Thomson explained in his original report.

The seal shares symbolism with the colors of the American flag. In addition, the **number thirteen** — denoting the thirteen original states — is represented in the bundle of arrows, the stripes of the shield, and the stars of the constellation. The constellation of stars symbolizes a new nation taking its place among other sovereign states. The motto *E Pluribus Unum* (Out of many, one), emblazoned across the scroll and clenched in the eagle's beak expresses the union of the thirteen States.